Thomas Toke Lynch

The Rivulet

A Contribution to Sacred Song. Fifth Edition

Thomas Toke Lynch

The Rivulet
A Contribution to Sacred Song. Fifth Edition

ISBN/EAN: 9783744768856

Printed in Europe, USA, Canada, Australia, Japan

Cover: Foto ©Thomas Meinert / pixelio.de

More available books at **www.hansebooks.com**

THE RIVULET:

A

CONTRIBUTION TO SACRED SONG.

BY

THOMAS T. LYNCH.

Fifth Edition.

'He shall drink of the brook in the way: therefore shall he lift up the head."

JAMES CLARKE AND CO.
13 & 14, FLEET STREET, LONDON.
1883.

LONDON:
PRINTED BY J. S. VIRTUE AND CO., LIMITED,
CITY ROAD.

PREFACE.

THE streams of sacred song make glad the City of God. They are, too, streams in the desert; and many who are weary and athirst as they travel towards the City, drinking of a brook by the way, can go on that way rejoicing.

Christian poetry is indeed a river of the water of life; and to this river my "Rivulet" brings its contribution, desiring in its individual course to afford such benefits as it may, and to augment, however little, that stream which, that it may ever fertilise the Christian country and ever refresh its people, must be itself ever fed by new supplies.

These HYMNS FOR HEART AND VOICE are suitable for the chamber or the church, and they may be "said or sung." Some of them are obviously more the expression of united worship than others. I have not separated these into a distinct group. They occupy what seemed to me suitable places in the general arrangement. Such hymns when read privately have often a peculiar charm: they connect us with those from whom we are parted, but with whom we are present in spirit; they make us feel that in the fellowship of the truth lies much of the power of the truth.

The book is, then, one of short Christian Poems, to peruse, as I hope, for stimulus and solace, or to sing in family and social communion. I shall be very glad and thankful, if in this case too, as in others, it be found true that "both is best."

> A Rivulet singing as it flows along
> Lulls us to rest, or thus invites a song:
> "New waters from the ancient fount I bring,
> That they who drink of me with me may sing."

THOMAS T. LYNCH.

KENTISH TOWN, LONDON,
November, 1855.

INDEX OF FIRST LINES.

	PAGE
Above the dusky air	24
A bubble I would be, says one	191
Again from mid-winter	128
Ah, miserable man	17
A little sunshine and a little talk	158
All faded is the glowing light	111
Aloft in the quietest air	8
Amid the hills retired	12
A mighty wind arose in air	148
Another day may bring another mind	122
Appear, O Thou, who very present art	200
Arise, sad heart, arise in haste	137
Arising, we sing	184
As one who for a letter waits	169
As to a quiet valley	103
As we by successive stages	73
As with sunny showers of song	57
A thousand years have come and gone	126
Behold, how mighty truth	112
Beneath the darkest, basest will	131
Be thy word with power fraught	105
Bread art Thou, by thy coming down	189
Breathe on us for the passing day	96
Brethren, let us to the Lord	23
Can a trustless thought intrude	49
Christ in his word draws near	19
Close not, ye heavens, that opened were	37
Come forth with twice-anointed feet	136
Creator, lover of the whole	181

INDEX OF FIRST LINES.

	PAGE
Day is passing, night is nigh	53
Departing in peace	118
Dismiss me not thy service, Lord	2
Fallen from ancestral glory	61
Father, what portion of thy goods	87
Flowers will not cease to speak	7
Folded close the shadows are	35
Forget not: can the mother's love	194
From each dark branchlet of the trees	75
Give Him brain and breast	161
Giver of sleep, unsleeping Lord	196
God of the shining sun	186
Gracious Spirit, dwell with me	65
Heart of Christ, O cup most golden	86
Heart with heart, and hand in hand	173
Help, holy Lord, against the league	149
Here are we dark and weak, yet are we not	202
He sat upon the mountain-side	145
How calmly the evening once more is descending	24
How can I sing?	183
How firmly they stand	77
How holy and secure those angels kind	201
How often on a morning bright	100
How sweet to me is life when shadows gray	203
If love in any heart arise	163
I give myself to prayer	47
I have looked above me	4
In silence mighty things are wrought	110
In the fellowship of song	80
In the time of our youth	31
In well-loved blue the heaven shines	144
Irresolute, I stand perplext	26
Is life a groping and a guess	46
I travelled upwards to the stars	166
I walked on sands beside the sea	71
Jesus, great friend of open speech	56
Jordan, O thou crooked river	139

INDEX OF FIRST LINES.

	PAGE
King of darkness, King of light	70
Let children come	176
Let us, with a wind-like song	41
Lift up your heads, rejoice	198
Like one who blind sits rushes weaving	107
Look up; the rainy heavens withdraw	14
Lord, all things everywhere	21
Lord, break the deadly battle-blow	44
Lord, how wonderful is man	99
Lord, I on every day	69
Lord of that undistracted realm	72
Lord, oft the heavens of day and night	40
Lord, on thy returning day	68
Lord, when in silent hours I muse	16
Lord, why dost Thou thy love conceal	49
Love me, O Lord, forgivingly	13
Most high and patient God	118
Mountains by the darkness hidden	108
My faith, it is an oaken staff	63
My hastening life admonishes	11
My little flower, my little flower	159
My soul, humility her fears have taught her	177
My work appointed I have done	91
Not afar from surf and wave	187
Now have we met that we may ask	55
O baby, He loved pretty things	175
O, break my heart; but break it as a field	10
O day of rest for busy men	178
Oft when of God we ask	106
O God, our spirits unassisted	89
O hand, O breath divine	141
O holy ones, O watchers calm	54
O, is the heart too soon appeased	15
O little one who art so great	125
O Lord, Thou art not fickle	59
O morning so bright	66
One blessing is there of the sun	180
One sat with angry heart alone	192

INDEX OF FIRST LINES.

	PAGE
One says, "The glow of life is over"	33
O, rest awhile, but only for a while	74
O, there are words lips often say	157
O Thou, who by the meat and drink	79
O Thou whose inmost name is Love	147
Our heart is like a little pool	82
O, were I ever what I am sometimes	114
O, where is He that trod the sea	42
O wondrous, weary years	127
Praying by the river-side	174
Remember us who would aright	152
Rise! He calleth thee, arise!	18
Say not, my soul, from whence	9
See, bannered armies hem	94
See multitudes surrounding	83
See the tide as advancing it breaks on the shingle	58
See, through the heavenly arch	34
Shadows now are darker growing	101
Since penalties so fearful	93
Slow is the fall to winter dark	84
Sometimes God lights his temple up	193
Speak not in the shaking thunder	27
Spirit of beauty, thy presence confessing	102
Spirit of sacred happiness	90
Spirit! whose various energies	1
The apostle spake of judgment just	143
The brooks that brim with showers	42
The chrysalis in crannies lies	116
The dewy flowers, more beautiful	51
The glory of God from the way of the East	140
The lengthening light leads on the year	51
The Lord is rich and merciful	179
There is purpose in this waste	135
The sacred word, so fraught with use	20
The sere leaf flickers down	116
The soul's sweet summer is not here	115
The sufferer had been heard to say	6
The sun aloft, but not aloof	151
The world was dark with care and woe	123

INDEX OF FIRST LINES.

	PAGE
Thou shalt not doubt the King most high	37
To-day they know not what they do	135
Together for our country now we pray	170
Weak we are, although sincere	97
We come, but not with sighs alone	170
We come to the place of our rest	81
We use or waste the beams so bright	155
What! is this the only rest?	133
What tears are these that flow so fast?	132
When Dorcas worked to clothe the poor	164
When fragrantly towards the skies	190
When happy Christian hope began	120
When strength is shaken and I fail	28
When the clouds so soft and tender	76
When the wind is blowing	38
Where is the stream, the happy stream	30
Where is thy God, my soul?	60
While the law on stone is written	29
While waiting for the summer sun	190
Wisdom coming from above	85
With feet of burning brass	121
With many a swift and crashing stroke	199
Who will roll away the stone?	134
Why stooped the Majesty on high?	160

INDEX OF TITLES.

	PAGE		PAGE
Admonition	192	Departure	118
Age	158	Discontent	87
Angels	201	Discretion	56
Anni Domini	127	Divine Fire	121
Another day	122	Dorcas	164
Ardour	31	Doubt not	37
A reasoner without love	17		
Ascension	144	Earth clothed anew	75
Autumn	116	Effort	58
		Emmanuel	160
Baby	175	Evening	24
Before sermon	105	Evil as Usurper	70
Benediction	145	Exhortation	179
Be strong	38	Expectation	111
Birth	186	Exultation	193
Brightness	100		
		Faith	63
Cheerfulness	42	Fellowship	81
Christ in his word	19	Flowers I.	49
Citizenship	61	Flowers II.	51
Cloudless night	72	Forget not	194
Comfort	15	Forgiving Love	13
Condescension	147	Foundations	77
Contrasts	99	Frailty	28
Courage	27	Freedom	116
Daybreak	18	Gleams	37

INDEX OF TITLES.

	PAGE
Glimpses	107
God our Home	46
God's Answers	106
Gone!	159
Hallelujah!	21
Health	30
Heart of Christ	86
Heaven	184
Help is sure	169
Holy Communion	152
Hope	24
Inconstancy	114
Infant Baptism	174
Intercession	170
Jerusalem	94
Jordan	139
Judgment	143
Law	29
Let children come	176
Life of our life	1
Loneliness	49
Marriage	173
Matins	181
Meditation	16
Midnight	54
Miracles	42
Morning	66
Neighbours	59
Night	53
Offerings	190
Old and New	96
One Family. Eph. iii. 14, 15	202
Onward and Upward	73
Panting after God	4
Patience	118
Patriotism	170
Penitence	135
Perplexity	26
Peter's Tears	132
Pleading	200
Prayer	47
Prayer for a broken heart	10
Prayer for the Holy Spirit	65
Privacy. Mark i. 32—38	35
Progress	212
Protection	93
Quiet	103
Rain	180
Reaping	120
Recovery	33
Relief	9
Renewal	76
Replies	183
Repose	82
Rescue	149
Rest	74
Restoration	203
Resurrection	157
Sabbath	68
Sacred Happiness	90
Scripture	20
Serenity	14
Service	2
Shadows	101
Showers of Song	57
Signs	198
Silence	110
Sin overcome	131
Singing	80
Sleep	196
Songs	41

INDEX OF TITLES.

Title	PAGE
Sorrow ended	137
Spirit of Beauty	102
Spring	51
Stars	34
Success	89
Succour	6
Sustenance	79
Sympathy	187
Tempest	199
Testimonies	163
The Bread of Life	189
The Child. Isa. ix. 6.	123
The Coming Summer	115
The Fount of Life	83
The Good News	126
The Heavens	40
The New Year	128
The Prize	191
The Risen Lord	141
The Softened Heart	8
The Son of the Highest. Luke i. 32	125
The Sower	178
The Spices	135
The Stone	134
The Stream of Love	12
The Sun	151
The Tomb	133
The Two Crowns	136
The Wanderer	166
Thoroughness	161
To arms!	23
Triumph	140
Unbelief	155
Unbelief forbidden	108
Victory	55
Voices in Nature	7
Waiting	190
Walking by the Sea	71
War	44
Waves	177
Weak though sincere	97
Week-day	69
Where is thy God?	60
Winds	148
Winter	84
Wisdom	85
Work	91
Zeal	11

O that, partaker of that sweet content
  Which all who in thy love believe have known,
I may the primal blessing Thou hast sent,
  The dove-like peace enjoy, which from thy throne

Forth-issuing visits every trusting heart,
  To give to it the sign of that communion
In which the great and small alike have part,
  Knowing each other in the same high union.

Of heart to Thee, the first, the universal,
  The great, the hidden one, yet the revealed;
Then here my song shall be a true rehearsal
  Of melodies which heavenly voices yield,

That celebrate the good of everything
  Which round about with various appealing
Offers thy love, Thou all-providing King,
  Its ever growing gift each day revealing.

"O, come, let us sing unto the Lord."

HYMNS FOR HEART AND VOICE.

I.

LIFE OF OUR LIFE.

SPIRIT ! whose various energies
    By dew and flame denoted are,
By rain from the world-covering skies,
    By rushing and by whispering air;

Be Thou to us, O gentlest one,
    The brimful river of sweet peace,
Sunshine of the celestial sun,
    Restoring air of sacred ease.

Life of our life, since life of Him
    By whom we live eternally,
Our heart is faint, our eye is dim,
    Till Thou our spirit purify.

The purest airs are strongest too,
    Strong to enliven and to heal:
O Spirit purer than the dew,
    Thine holiness in strength reveal.

Felt art Thou, and the heavy heart
  Grows cheerful and makes bright the eyes;
Up from the dust the enfeebled start,
  Armed and re-nerved for victories:

Felt art Thou, and relieving tears
  Fall, nourishing our young resolves:
Felt art Thou, and our icy fears
  The sunny smile of love dissolves.

O Spirit, when thy mighty wind
  The entombing rocks of sin hath rent,
Lead shuddering forth the awakened mind,
  In still voice whispering thine intent.

As to the sacred light of day
  The stranger soul shall trembling come,
Say, "These thy friends," and "This thy way,"
  And "Yonder thy celestial home."

II.

SERVICE.

Dismiss me not thy service, Lord,
  But train me for thy will;
For even I in fields so broad
  Some duties may fulfil;
And I will ask for no reward,
  Except to serve Thee still.

How many serve, how many more
    May to the service come;
To tend the vines, the grapes to store,
    Thou dost appoint for some:
Thou hast thy young men at the war,
    Thy little ones at home.

All works are good, and each is best
    As most it pleases Thee;
Each worker pleases when the rest
    He serves in charity:
And neither man nor work unblest
    Wilt thou permit to be.

O ye who serve, remember One
    The worker's way who trod;
He served as man, but now his throne,
    It is the throne of God:
The sceptre He hath to us shown
    Is like a blossoming rod.

Firm fibres of the tree of life
    Hath each command of his,
And each with clustering blossoms rife
    At every season is;
Bare only, like a sword of strife,
    Against love's enemies.

Our Master all the work hath done
    He asks of us to-day;
Sharing his service, every one
    Share too his sonship may.
Lord, I would serve and be a son;
    Dismiss me not, I pray.

III.

PANTING AFTER GOD.

I HAVE looked above me,
    Saying as I stood,
"Shall I ever love Thee
    Even as I would?"
Hands together clasping,
    Prayer to Thee I urge;
Like a swimmer gasping
    In the ocean surge.

I for love endeavour
    As for breath of life;
Must I seek it ever
    With a painful strife?
I on waves of thinking
    Foothold cannot keep;
Downward am I sinking,
    Over me they sweep.

Lord, Thou art above me,
    Silent and serene;
Surely I could love Thee,
    If I once had seen
Christ as Saviour ready
    Fearful hearts to save;
Giving footsteps steady
    Even on the wave.

Is He coming near me?
    Will He by me stand?
Will He speak and cheer me,
    Take me by the hand?
May the humble-minded
    See Him on his way,
Though the proud are blinded
    By the fretful spray?

O, if I but know Thee
    In thy human form;
O, if Thou but show me
    Jesus in the storm;
Perils never counting,
    In love's air I'll breathe;
Hugest doubts surmounting,
    Though they cry and seethe.

IV.

SUCCOUR.

The sufferer had been heard to say,
  "I am the unhappiest in the land;"
But comforted went on his way,
  When Jesus took him by the hand.

The poor man had been oft passed by
  By many people rich and grand;
But found at last prosperity,
  When Jesus took him by the hand.

The sinner in unpitied blame
  Was perishing, an outcast banned;
But rose, and left behind his shame,
  When Jesus took him by the hand.

And many of whom all men said,
  "They've fallen never more to stand,"
Have risen, though they seemed as dead,
  When Jesus took them by the hand.

O ye, who in the journey's length
  Must often tread the weary sand,
Your fainting limbs will gather strength,
  If Jesus takes you by the hand.

"Come unto me," the Saviour cries,
  Nor speaks in accents falsely bland:
"Hard is the way," He says, "but rise:"
  And then He takes us by the hand.

V.

VOICES IN NATURE.

Flowers will not cease to speak,
    And tell the praise of God,
Even to the careless man
    Who has upon them trod:
Rising suns and falling rain
    Will not refuse their gift to yield,
Though of our neglect complain
    The garden and the field:

Birds will not refuse to sing
    The summer woods among,
Though we to their God and ours
    No song have ever sung:
Heaven will not at once grow dim,
    Because unhonoured by a look;
Nor the temple close on him
    Who worship has forsook.

Whether we are thine or no,
    Thy mercies, Lord, are ours;
And thy choicest works and words
    Still breathe on us their powers;
They, by victory of love,
    Can move the hardened to relent;
They have voices from above,
    To call us upward sent.

VI.

THE SOFTENED HEART.

Aloft in the quietest air
    Serenely the cloudlets repose;
The God who has made them so fair,
    His love in their loveliness shows.
It rests us to look on their calm;
    Their softness can soften our heart;
Our hurry, distress, and alarm,
    They silently tell to depart.

Like raiment of angels they shine;
    No fingers such robes ever spun;
Their texture so airily fine
    Is dyed in the hues of the sun:
Such garments for souls may be had,
    On us the like glory appear;
In gentleness may we be clad,
    And rectitude winningly clear.

The light of religion, that flows
    From robes that our spirits desire,
Is warm, though as white as the snows,
    And mild, though as ruddy as fire.
Lord, clothe us in sanctity bright;
    Let love with its zest and its zeal
Be mingling the red and the white,
    And Christ in our aspect reveal.

VII.

RELIEF.

Say not, my soul, " From whence
    Can God relieve my care?"
Remember that Omnipotence
    Has servants everywhere:
But if as weak and poor
    Thou seekest charity,
Christ may come knocking at thy door,
    And ask relief of thee.

He comes as truth denied,
    Comes as a wounded heart;
Sees if with courage well supplied
    And kindliness thou art.
Will He an alms receive?
    Then never doubt and fret;
Is He less able to relieve,
    More likely to forget?

God's help is always sure,
    His methods seldom guessed;
Delay will make our pleasure pure,
    Surprise will give it zest:
His wisdom is sublime,
    His heart profoundly kind;
God never is before his time,
    And never is behind.

Hast thou assumed a load
    Which few will share with thee,
  And art thou carrying it for God,
    And shall He fail to see?
  Be comforted at heart,
    Thou art not left alone:
  Now thou the Lord's companion art;
    Soon thou wilt share his throne.

VIII.

PRAYER FOR A BROKEN HEART.

O, BREAK my heart; but break it as a field
  Is by the plough up-broken for the corn:
O, break it as the buds, by green leaf sealed,
  Are, to unloose the golden blossom, torn:
Love would I offer unto love's great Master,
Set free the odour, break the alabaster.

O, break my heart; break it, victorious God,
That life's eternal well may flash abroad:
O, let it break as when the captive trees,
Breaking cold bonds, regain their liberties:
And as thought's sacred grove to life is springing,
Be joys, like birds, their hope thy victory singing.

IX.

ZEAL.

My hastening life admonishes
    My often-faltering soul to try
And yet perform some goodly work,
    Ere, with the years, desires fly.

What, in a world where cries for help
    Must ever sound till sin shall cease,
Can be a goodlier work than this,—
    Griefs to assuage, and joys increase?

To fill with light some sunken eyes
    Where reason struggles with despair:
To bring sin's pallid prisoners forth
    Into the free and wholesome air:

To cheer the oppressed with righteous words,
    And aid them with a labouring arm:
The slaves of tyrant ignorance
    To rescue, and then shield, from harm:

To offer cups of water pure
    From rocky truth's cool, plenteous well,
To souls confused with feverish woes
    Unspoken and unspeakable:

To set ablaze some signal-fire
    Of zealous thought, till in affright
The careless slumberers start and rise,
    And rally round the true and right.

Let me remeditate the truth,
   That Christ did for and with us bleed,
Then, " He is good that doeth good,"
   Shall be my dear and honoured creed.

O, if no partner in the pains
   By which love labours for my race,
Death, that takes home and crowns the brave,
   Can but insure my long disgrace.

X.

THE STREAM OF LOVE.

Amid the hills retired
   A fount began its flow,
And riches soon acquired
   To bless the lands below;
And though its wealth it freely spent,
It grew the richer as it went.

For solitary hills,
   From stores of rain and snow,
Contributed new rills,
   Their sympathy to show;
And soon the river on the plains
As monarch of their plenty reigns.

Our God in hours retired
   Can open in our heart

A fount of good desired,
   And such supplies impart,
That more it has, the more it gives,
And all our life upon it lives.

O sacred stream of love,
   Hast thou begun thy flow,
And from the hills above
   Reached now the lands below?
Then, blessed by thee, life's common field
Will corn and fruit and herbage yield.

XI.

FORGIVING LOVE.

Love me, O Lord, forgivingly,
   O, ever be my friend;
And still, when Thou reprovest me,
   Reproof with pity blend.

O, pity me when weak I fall;
   And as with saddened eyes
I upwards look, O, let thy call
   Come strengthening me to rise.

My sins, dispersed by mercy bright,
   Like clouds again grow black;
O, change the winds that bring such night,
   And drive the darkness back.

This striving weather, let it cease;
    Then fervent, fruitful days
Shall yield both promise and increase,
    And make my growth thy praise.

XII.

SERENITY.

Look up; the rainy heavens withdraw,
    Light flows anew at ebb of day;
Look, and believe the gracious law,
    That love shall have the final sway.

The grass is of a perfect green,
    Dappled with shades this pleasant hour;
The garden-walk is crisp and clean;
    Wind shakes the tears from bough and flower.

Its finest life is in the air,
    Its finest lustre in the light;
And see! the drifting clouds of care
    Are touched with glory in their flight.

In such an hour is understood
    The sacred mystery of woe;
We feel a life divinely good
    Within us rise, around us flow:

A spirit tranquil as of one
    Who finds in happy languor rest,
Sore wearied with his work well done,
    But through well-doing richly blest:

A spirit as of one who broods
    On sorrows ceased but unforgot;
Whose heart, like heaven, the rainiest moods
    Leave softer, and without a blot.

Come, holy peace, when evening's flame
    Burns in the west intensely still,
Come, kindling salutary shame
    For half-won good, half-vanquished ill.

XIII.

COMFORT.

O, is the heart too soon appeased,
O, is its pain too lightly eased,
When, though the sun with stinted ray
Has been but glimmering all the day,
One last brief gush of glory bright
Can fill and flood it with delight?

No; to the heart this beam so brief
Pledges, as well as brings, relief;
Light from serene eternity
Now flushes promise through the sky,

That thus shall life, its dark day spent,
End in an ocean of content.

When once our cloudy course has run,
The long-obscured but waiting sun
In morning might and evening peace
Shall shine, and as our labours cease,
Our craving spirits fully bless
With quick, triumphant happiness.

O glorious truth! and is it true
For me, my Lord, whose hopes are few,
Whose chiefest grief and fault it is
That proffered hopes he makes not his?
One sunny gush of comfort give;
O, say again, "Believe, and live."

XIV.

MEDITATION.

LORD, when in silent hours I muse
    Upon myself and Thee,
I seem to hear the stream of life
    That runs invisibly.

Then know I, what I oft forget,
    How fleeting are my days;
Remember me, my God, nor let
    My end be my dispraise.

O, think upon me for my good,
    Though little good I do;
My hope, and my forgiving friend,
    Thou hast been hitherto.

And I would live in such a course,
    That men to me may say,
" O, whence hast thou thy joy and force,
    What is thy secret stay?"

My joy, when truest joy I have,
    It comes to me from heaven;
My strength, when I from weakness rise,
    Is by thy Spirit given.

And while He shines as He has shone
    Whom Thou hast made my stay,
Life can but gently float me on,
    Not hurry me away.

XV.

A REASONER WITHOUT LOVE.

AH, miserable man,
    What feeble taper light
Is this, which casts its spectral gleam
    Into the murky night?

A reasoner without love,
    Thy quivering ray forlorn
Can show the strange and fearful night,
    But never bring the dawn.

Lord, in our musing heart
    If Thou reveal thy Son,
Upward the growing twilight strikes,
    The morning has begun.

The orb of love appears,
    Night and its dreams are o'er;
In such a light need never man
    Be miserable more.

XVI.

DAYBREAK.

RISE! He calleth thee, arise!
    Come, O sorrow-blinded man;
He who lighted first the eyes,
    Only He relight them can.

Come, and see the face of one
    Who familiar was with grief;
Now it shineth as the sun;
    In his smile is thy relief.

Rise! He calleth thee, arise!
    Prisoner of an inward night;
Sin destroyeth earth and skies,
    If it quench the fount of light.

Come, of daybreak 'tis the hour
    When thou seest Christ the Lord;
See Him, and regain the power
    Both to look and walk abroad.

XVII.

CHRIST IN HIS WORD.

CHRIST in his word draws near;
Hush, moaning voice of fear,
    He bids thee cease:
With songs sincere and sweet
Let us arise, and meet
Him who comes forth to greet
    Our souls with peace.

Rising above thy care,
Meet Him as in the air,
    O weary heart:
Put on joy's sacred dress,
Lo, as He comes to bless,
Quite from thy weariness
    Set free thou art.

For works of love and praise
He brings thee summer days,
   Warm days and bright:
Winter is past and gone,
Now He, salvation's sun,
Shineth on every one
   With mercy's light.

From the bright sky above,
Clad in his robes of love,
   'Tis He, our Lord:
Dim earth itself grows clear
As his light draweth near:
O, let us hush and hear
   His holy word.

XVIII.

SCRIPTURE.

The sacred word, so fraught with use,
   Is bright with beauty too,
Oft startling us like blooms profuse
   Upon a sudden view.

But more amazing than the bloom
   Which all the tree bestuds,
See, peering from the leafy gloom,
   A hundred thousand buds.

O, bud for ever, glorious tree,
  O, ever blossom thus;
So shall thy good fruits plenteously
  Hang ripening for us.

XIX.

HALLELUJAH!

Lord, all things everywhere
Thy mighty praise declare;
Some may muse, and some may sing,
But they all are worshipping:
Or by silence or by sound
Thou art praised the world around.

Ever the circling earth
Gives night and morning birth;
Every moment some place knows
Work returning or repose;
Some things wake, and some things rest;
But by all thy love is blest.

The stormy seas and calm
Join in a giant psalm,
Solemn praises unto Thee
Sounding forth unceasingly:
Verses loud and verses low
Equally thy glory show.

The rooted mountains grand
All reverently stand,
And by silent awe express
Lowly-hearted loftiness;
Sometimes veiled, and sometimes bare,
Now for praises, now for prayer.

How doth the ample sky
Shine with thy majesty!
Sun and stars in every clime
Keep their course and change their time;
And by sunshine or by shower
Thou art honoured every hour.

Still with unchanging plan
Thou blessest wayward man,
And the varying hours prove
That Thou hast unvarying love:
Sometimes grieved and sometimes gay,
We would trust Thee every day.

Lord, shall sin work Thee shame,
To cloud thy glorious Name?
No, Thou art so good and just,
Sin and sorrow serve Thee must:
While they last and when they die,
Thou art hope, Thou victory.

The cross and sepulchre
On love the crown confer;

Suffering has vanquished pain,
Dying has made death a gain :
Wicked hands but wrought their deed,
That a Saviour might succeed.

XX.

TO ARMS !

BRETHREN, let us to the Lord
Give ourselves, both heart and sword;
Under his commanding eye
We shall march to victory.

Hark, the strains of music roll,
Like a tide they fill the soul ;
As they to their highest rise,
We will launch our enterprise.

Ye who 'list must 'list in faith,
Fearing neither toil nor scath ;
Calm mid the bewildering cry,
Confident of victory.

Hark, the music loud and sweet
Thrills our heart and stirs our feet :
Brethren, hands upon our swords,
Let us shout, " We are the Lord's ! "

XXI.

EVENING.

How calmly the evening once more is descending,
    As kind as a promise, as still as a prayer;
O wing of the Lord, in thy shelter befriending
    May we and our households continue to share!

The sky, like the kingdom of heaven, is open;
    O, enter, my soul, at the glorious gates;
The silence and smile of his love are the token,
    Who now for all comers invitingly waits.

We come to be soothed with his merciful healing,
    The dews of the night cure the wounds of the day;
We come, our life's worth and its brevity feeling,
    With thanks for the past, for the future we pray.

Lord, save us from folly; be with us in sorrow;
    Sustain us in work till the time of our rest;
When earth's day is over, may heaven's to-morrow
    Dawn on us, of homes long expected possest.

XXII.

HOPE.

Above the dusky air
    Shine the bright steps of hope;
And I, though from the lowest stair,
    Would mount to heaven's cope.

Thus yearning, I arise,
   But heavily I move :
Alas that, with such wistful eyes,
   My limbs so feeble prove !

O thou essential Light,
   How can I climb to Thee?
The starry way is infinite—
   My hope is vanity.

Ah, glorious vanity!
   It is as if the sun
Were quenched in waves, as from the sea
   His upward course begun.

But can the morning fail,
   Though dawn be dark and wild ?
Rejoice, O soul, thou shalt prevail ;
   Of light thou art the child.

So shall thy hope be made
   Thy strength, if it be bright ;
Thy limbs, so heavy in the shade,
   Grow lighter in the light.

XXIII.

PERPLEXITY.

Irresolute, I stand perplext,
What pathway shall I follow next?
Show me the way that I must take;
Show me, O Lord, for Jesus' sake.

He is the upward way for all,
Upon whose steep ascents there fall
Sweet lustres from the gates above,
The ever-open gates of love.

I know Him: but when thus I stay,
And musing loiter time away,
A shadow dims that sacred light
Which shines to guide from height to height.

Unless some earthly way I take,
I cannot heavenward progress make;
With settled aim and conscience clear,
What shall I do? how journey here?

My soul the untried seas would dare,
Or sands of every way-mark bare,
Should but thy voice distinctly say,
"Go forward, soul; there lies thy way."

Say, "This thou *must* do:" such behest
Can make the darkest path the best:
If but I know my way through time,
My soul those sunny steeps can climb.

XXIV.

COURAGE.

Speak not in the shaking thunder,
    Shine not in the lightning's blaze;
Mercy's heaven we still are under,
    O thou God of wise delays:
Mercy's angels still attend us,
    Breathing helpful winds from Thee;
Save us from the surge tremendous
    Of destruction's angry sea.

Fill us with the love, outcasting
    Murmur, fearfulness, and sleep:
Towards the city everlasting,
    Night and day across the deep,
With a steady will unswerving,
    Ship-like may we onward press,
Buoyant mastery preserving
    O'er the watery wilderness.

Then if winds, their trumpets blowing,
    Summon all the waves to rise,
Faith to her perfection growing,
    Mid her wrestling agonies,
Thus shall cry, "O Father, hearken;
    Thou hast saved, and still wilt save;
Love has bid this tempest darken,
    Love would have his children brave."

Storms shall but our heart embolden;
    Sweet returns the assuring sun;
Under heavens calm and golden
    Peacefully we prosper on;
Wrecking judgments never fearing,
    Now with heart unmutinous,
Under orders, we are nearing
    Homes God has prepared for us.

XXV.

FRAILTY.

WHEN strength is shaken and I fail,
    My pain subduing me,
I see the trembling of the vail
    That hides eternity:
The unlifted curtain only shakes,
But this the future present makes.

How near, how real, the hidden scene!
    Disclosure soon may come;
Only a curtain lies between
    Me and my final home:
My home! ah, till I so can say,
My God, permit me here to stay.

O, who would wish to enter fresh
    Earth's dark and troubled land?
What if a world behind the flesh
    Yet worse than earth there stand!

Lord, of a better world we sing;
Thither Thou wouldst our spirits bring.

Like glimmers of the light of heaven
    That struggle through the vail,
Let truth be felt, and joy be given,
    In hours when we are frail:
Love can our spirits tranquillise,
Whether the curtain shake or rise.

XXVI.

LAW.

WHILE the law on stone is written,
    Stone-like is the mighty word;
We with chilling awe are smitten,
    Though the word is thine, O Lord.
Firm it is as mountains old,
As their snowy summits cold.

Stone-like, too, on each offender
    Broken laws may heavy fall,
And with crushing vengeance render
    One a terror unto all:
Struck themselves, in enmity,
Ireful sparks may from them fly.

Lord, Thou hast the law re-written,
    Where we may untrembling read
We with tender awe are smitten,
    As we see the Saviour bleed,—

Bleed in his obedient love,
Hope and zeal in us to move.

From his heart the law is shining,
    Heart-like is its every word;
We who in the cold were pining,
    Of the sunny warmth have heard:
From the rocks we feared would crush
At his touch sweet waters gush.

Honoured be the name of Jesus,
    Who for us obedient stood;
Faith in Him from fear will ease us,
    Love to Him will make us good:
When the law in love is shown,
Hearts we have instead of stone.

XXVII.

HEALTH.

"Where is the stream, the happy stream,
    To rid me of distempering heat;
To lave me in its running strength,
    And give my heart a moderate beat?"

Streams not the wind, the breezy wind,
    In sunny currents by thy side?
The morning and the evening air,
    O, hast thou, and yet vainly, tried?

God bathes thee when heart-soothing air
    Ripples around thee easingly;
Then gently comes the grateful wish
    Yet to be his well-pleasingly.

Yet to be his, and ever his,
    The wistful heart in worship yearns;
When lighter grows the load of life,
    And injured happiness returns.

Inert in the sepulchral gloom
    Of dusky, spirit-palsying care,
Why shouldst thou lie, when liberal love
    Awaits thee in the open air?

Chained as thou art, thyself drag forth,
    Fevered and fettered, to the breeze:
Thy chains shall fall, thy heats subside,
    And the stream cleanse thee as it frees.

XXVIII.

ARDOUR.

In the time of our youth
    What a glory of truth
May encircle our brow as we muse!
    Never darksome the day;
    For, go whither we may,
We can brighten the light as we choose.

So intense and devout,
We are never without
Something great to be hoped for or done;
And are ready to bleed,
If we may but succeed,
And the battle for justice be won.

But this zeal may decay,
And our light fade away,
And the heart may grow misty and cold;
And the man at full age
Be too wise to engage
In a battle, excepting for gold.

What! is all thou hast done,
Flash thy sword in the sun,
And declare what thou one day wouldst do?
Hadst thou rather now see
All the world serving thee
Than by suffering serve God with the few?

Love's tower looked so high,
Seen by fancy's bright eye,
What a glorious structure to build!
But the cost proved too vast,
And the labour must last
All thy life: so thine ardour was chilled.

Saviour! who for the truth,
At the close of thy youth,
Camest forth, and didst wondrously fight;

Thou canst give what was thine,
    Love and ardour divine:
O, renew us our youth with its light!

XXIX.

RECOVERY.

ONE says, "The glow of life is over,
    The summer days are past;
The air no more is sweet with clover,
    Bitter is every blast."
Another says, "I too was fearful,
    And thought the summer gone;
But now am comforted and cheerful,
    Again the sun hath shone:

The sun hath shone, and now is shining,
    And, O, the subtle air—
A solace and a spur combining—
    With marvellous repair
Rebuilds my heart, that time had wasted,
    And all my hopes re-swell,
As if, when God began, He hasted
    To make our sickness well."

O, though for us is no returning
    Upon our former track,
The hopes for which our heart is yearning
    Are ever coming back:

Deep inward thrills break up inaction,
    And power we regain,
When by our Maker's benefaction
    Comes sunshine after rain.

XXX.

STARS.

SEE! through the heavenly arch
    With silent, stately march
The starry ranks for ever sweep;
    In graduate scale of might
    They all are sons of light,
And all their times and orders keep.

    O glorious, countless host,
    Which shall I praise the most?
Your lustrous groups, or course exact?
    Ye on your way sublime
    Defy confusing time
Your light to dim, your path distract.

    Earth's early fathers saw
    The gospel and the law
In the firm beauty of the skies:
    O thou unswerving Will,
    The unveiled heavens still
Show Thee as glorious, good, and wise.

Lord of the starry night,
With awe and with delight
Under thy temple dome we pray :
  Still as we gaze above,
  Temper our fear with love,
That we may filial homage pay.

  Not as the primal force
  Impelling nature's course,
We know Thee, but as Father dear:
  O, if with foolish mind
  We judge Thee weakly kind,
Correct false love with filial fear.

XXXI.

PRIVACY. Mark i. 32—38.

FOLDED close the shadows are,
And no disappearing star
Tells of morn, still distant far,
        Coming slowly on.

On his dusk and silent way,
Hark, the Lord goes forth to pray!
He whose mercies yesterday
        On the city shone.

Homes where late was sore distress
Now unusual slumbers bless;
Tired with very happiness
        Hush'd the sleepers lie.

He for strength must go alone,
See the sun ascend his throne,
Feel that symbol of his own
        Glorious victory.

Loneliness to Him is rest,
In his deep and open breast
Then arise those fountains blest
        By which earth is healed.

Now the day is bright and broad,
Crossing the still dewy sward
Strong to do the work of God,
        Lo, He stands revealed!

Coming from communings sweet
With his Father, see Him meet
The inquiring throng, and greet
        All with wisest love.

"Day advances; we must reach
Other cities, there to teach;
Far and wide good news to preach
        Came I from above."

XXXII.

GLEAMS.

CLOSE not, ye heavens, that opened were,
    And shone with such a gladdening light:
'Twas hard the unbroken dark to bear,
    But harder still re-gathering night.

O, shine with an abiding smile;
    Alone in your unspoken love
Have I sufficient solace while
    I struggle towards my home above.

Must smiles be brief? Then let there burn
    A light by fresh ones in my heart
Kindled and fed, till darkness turn
    To day that never can depart.

XXXIII.

DOUBT NOT.

THOU shalt not doubt the King most high,
    Whose glory is creation's good;
Sunlike his beams of majesty
    The storming ages have withstood.
The pillars of eternal right
    Who from their rocky hold can wrench?
The flame of the eternal light
    What gloom can hide, what wind can quench?

Thou shalt not doubt the awful King;
    Glory is his, but terror too;
The rebel storms their homage bring,
    And bow their pride his will to do.
If darkness is his judgment-dress,
    His sunny robes He will resume;
Unfailing He returns to bless,
    Like daybreak from the midnight's tomb.

Thou shalt not doubt eternal God;
    Mercy upholds his stately throne;
He wins creation's heart by blood;
    Our blood it is, and yet his own.
O solemn and consoling sign!
    Wilt thou be saved? He save thee will.
Thy blood was his; then his is thine;
    He in thee will thine hope fulfil.

XXXIV.

BE STRONG.

When the wind is blowing,
    Do not shrink and cower;
Firmly onward going,
    Feel the joy of power:
Heaviest the heart is
    In a heavy air;
Every wind that rises
    Blows away despair.

With the waves contending,
   See, the ships prevail,
Winning aid befriending
   From the adverse gale.
Thus the way contesting
   Souls must hold their course,
Thus a blessing wresting
   From each hostile force.

When the darts but rattle
   On the coward's shield,
He will quit the battle,
   Sword and self will yield:
From the fear of failing
   Shall we cease to pray?
On the foe's assailing
   Throw the shield away?

Hopeless, and yet winning,
   Thou wilt wiser be,
Wit's end the beginning
   Of new faith in thee:
Foes, and winds, and weather
   To confront resolve:
Faith and skill together
   Hardest problems solve.

XXXV.

THE HEAVENS.

Lord, oft the heavens of day and night,
    Shining as if to sanctify,
Seem so pathetically bright,
    I breathe a spiritual sigh.

The sigh of one who in unrest
    A moment shares the peace above;
The sigh of one who has been blest,
    And gently feels upbraiding love.

The sigh of one who, worn with strife,
    Has careless grown to further harm;
But, touched with former, happier life,
    Yearns now for an eternal calm.

Self-blamed, self-pitying, my heart
    Sighing suspects a sad reverse:
With joy I chose the better part;
    Can I have left it for the worse?

O, were I good as ye are bright,
    Ye heavens, that proffer sympathy;
And steadfast as your stars of light,
    Whose kingly look oft pierces me!

Lord, it is for that life I sigh
    Whose utmost glories are afar;
Oft trembling, when I feel it nigh,
    Lest sin and care my hope should mar.

XXXVI.

SONGS.

Let us, with a wind-like song
    Freshen all the air of life;
Singing makes the weak heart strong,
    Now to win seems worth the strife;
Songs to Him who is our light
    Will disperse each cloudy fear;
Songs to Him who is our might
    Will the wavering onward cheer.

Let us sing the solemn praise
    Of that blessed Potentate,
Who with life's eternal blaze
    Does the heavens irradiate:
He for ever, only He,
    Has a throne all thrones above;
Name his realm Immensity,
    Name the mighty ruler Love.

Songs to Thee, O mighty Love,
    Have a sound like coming rain,
Whose abundance soon shall prove
    Thou hast heard our souls complain.
O, forgive our murmurings, Lord;
    Think but of our thirsty hours;
From the bright clouds of thy word
    Let us now have balmy showers.

XXXVII.

CHEERFULNESS.

The brooks that brim with showers
    And sparkle on their way,
Will freshen and will feed the flowers;
    Thus working while they play.

Nor will our hearts do less,
    If happily we live;
For cheerfulness is usefulness,—
    The life we have we give.

Truth is a sacred rain,
    Our hearts but scanty rills,
Which higher power and pleasure gain
    As truth the current fills.

If freely we receive,
    We freely will bestow;
And tokens of our passage leave
    Where'er we shine and flow.

XXXVIII.

MIRACLES.

O, where is He that trod the sea,
    O, where is He that spake,—
And demons from their victims flee,
    The dead their slumbers break;

The palsied rise in freedom strong,
    The dumb men talk and sing,
And from blind eyes, benighted long,
    Bright beams of morning spring.

O, where is He that trod the sea,
    O, where is He that spake,—
And piercing words of liberty
    The deaf ears open shake;
And mildest words arrest the haste
    Of fever's deadly fire,
And strong ones heal the weak who waste
    Their life in sad desire.

O, where is He that trod the sea,
    O, where is He that spake,—
And dark waves, rolling heavily,
    A glassy smoothness take;
And lepers, whose own flesh has been
    A solitary grave,
See with amaze that they are clean,
    And cry, " 'Tis He can save!"

O, where is He that trod the sea,—
    'Tis only He can save;
To thousands hungering wearily
    A wondrous meal He gave:
Full soon, celestially fed,
    Their rustic fare they take;

'Twas springtide when He blest the bread,
And harvest when He brake.

O, where is He that trod the sea,—
　　My soul! the Lord is here:
Let all thy fears be hushed in thee;
　　To leap, to look, to hear,
Be thine: thy needs He'll satisfy:
　　Art thou diseased, or dumb?
Or dost thou in thine hunger cry?
　　"I come," saith Christ; "I come."

XXXIX.

WAR.

LORD, break the deadly battle-bow,
　　Unfold the glorious bow of peace,
And by that sign of mercy show
　　That war so merciless shall cease.

Lord, shut the cannon's gloomy mouth,
　　For ever hush its thundering tongue;
The risen sun must reach the south,
　　The songs of peace must yet be sung.

Fair peace shall be to truth at last,
　　Whose love for her no trouble quells,
Wedded indissolubly fast,
　　And earth shall hear the marriage-bells.

Yet, Lord, who wilt most surely hush
    The maddened world into a calm,
The mighty floods that whirl and rush
    Have wrought us good, amid their harm.

Thy judgment was a mercy then,
    When Thou didst purify the world,
And wicked works and wicked men
    One flood to common ruin hurled.

And often by confusions vast
    Hast Thou prepared thy blessings best;
Yet, Lord, how long? O, for the last
    Great strife, and then the final rest!

Come, thou Redeemer, whom we trust;
    Come, Jesus, gentle, though severe:
This have we learned,—we must be just,
    Then Thou wilt make thy peace appear.

Saviour, when thy bright love is shed
    On earth's innumerable tears,
Mercy's broad bow shall be outspread,
    The hope of sweet millennial years.

XL.

GOD OUR HOME.

Is life a groping and a guess,
A vain cry in a wilderness,
   No light of home at distance seen?
And do our hearts like fallen trees
Drift down the rivers to the seas,
   Though hope hath once exalted been?

We are not driftwood on the wave;
But like the ships, that tempests brave,
   Our hearts upon their voyage stand:
We utter no unheeded cry,
"Where is my God?" Lo, He is nigh,
   And says, "Take, child, thy Father's hand."

Must they who seek for wisdom be
Like mariners on a shoreless sea,
   Still circling round the water-world;
At last, exhausting heart and store,
To spring a leak, and, seen no more,
   To sink, though still with sail unfurled?

His soul a haven found for rest
Who leaned upon his Saviour's breast—
   An island mid the waters' foam:
But once at rest, lo, soon we are
At sea again, and Christ our star,
   And God our final port and home.

XLI.

PRAYER.

I GIVE myself to prayer;
    Lord, give Thyself to me,
And let the time of my request
    Thy time of answer be.

My thoughts are like the reeds,
    And tremble as they grow,
In the sad current of a life
    That darkly runs and slow.

No song is in the air,
    But one pervading fear;
Death's shadow dims my light, and Death
    Himself is lurking near.

I am as if asleep,
    Yet conscious that I dream;
Like one who vainly strives to wake
    And free himself, I seem.

The loud distressful cry
    With which I call on Thee,
Shall wake me, Lord, to find that Thou
    Canst give me liberty.

O, break this darksome spell,
　　This murky sadness strange;
Let me the terrors of the night
　　For cheerful day exchange.

Freshen the air with wind,
　　Comfort my heart with song;
Let thoughts be lilies pure, and life
　　A river bright and strong.

Save me from subtle Death,
　　Who, serpent-like, by fear
Palsies me for escape, yet draws
　　His trembling victim near.

I give myself to prayer;
　　Lord, give Thyself to me;
And in the time of my distress,
　　O, haste and succour me.

Then be my heart, my world,
　　Re-hallowed unto Thee,
And thy pervading glory, Lord,
　　O, let me feel and see.

XLII.

LONELINESS.

Lord, why dost Thou thy love conceal,
    And why so long a silence keep?
When souls by Thee forsaken feel,
    Childlike, they tremble and they weep;

Or stand in mute and tearless woe
    Like crosses, which their victims leave,
And which no more the sufferer show,
    But tell of grief, yet do not grieve.

O Lord, when darkest grows the hour,
    And loneliest feels the childlike heart,
Then show Thyself in sudden power
    To be the Father that Thou art.

And when the rigid heart but seems
    A monument of former woe,
Reveal love's meaning in extremes,
    And crosses trees of life shall grow.

XLIII.

FLOWERS.—I.

Can a trustless thought intrude,
While I stand in gratitude
Looking at you, O sweet flowers,
Prophets still of happy hours?

True it is I gaze and sigh,
So uncouth and darksome I;
But I should not love you so,
Could I not more lovely grow.

Though it may not yet be seen
What ye severally mean,
As by alphabetic speech
Though ye can no wisdom teach;

Yet ye seem to sing a strain
Into joy converting pain;
And our creeping thoughts arise
Winged for sunny ecstasies.

O, what forms and tints have ye,
Nature's living jewelry;
And though each of beauty rare,
Yet how plentiful ye are!

Happy are the pure, whose heart
Freely blooms in every part;
Godly acts are living gems,
Fit for crowns and diadems.

XLIV.

FLOWERS.—II.

The dewy flowers, more beautiful
    For tears upon their open face,
Gaze on us as from hearts brimful
    Of tender pity for our case.

Pitying they look, and yet as sure
    That not without good hope we are;
Will we not patiently endure?
    Help cannot now be distant far.

Help is not far, ye tender flowers,
    Whose beauty must so soon be past;
For God hath gifted you with powers
    To help us while your blossoms last.

Help while they last? O, yes, and when
    Their colour fades, their leaflets dry,
Remembering ye must bloom again,
    Help have we in that memory.

XLV.

SPRING.

The lengthening light leads on the year
From flushing spring towards autumn sere,
And all the marvels have begun
That wait upon the strengthening sun:
And spring has of those plants the power
Whose earliest blades enclose a flower.

Now brighter hues and clearer light
Are later lingering every night.
Sing, heart! with an adoring sense
Of nature's new magnificence:
O, look not on the glowing sky
Without a childlike ecstasy.

Spring so with strength her sweetness blends,
Our heart its wintry covering rends:
We have been, may we yet be, glad?
May former vantage still be had;
Have we this year another prime,
To countervail our misused time?

Now earth seems by the heavens above
Bewept with wonderment and love:
O heaven, thy prodigal embrace,
Show him the old maternal face;
Thy love, unlost! his fear relieves,
At his own happiness he grieves.

My God, in nature I confess
A beauty fraught with holiness;
Love-written, plainly I descry
My life's commandment in the sky:
O, still to me the days endear
When lengthening light leads on the year.

In pity and benignity,
Saviour, O, fully shine on me;

And as thy beams upon me glow,
Their power within me I would show:
May clustering actions on that vine,
My heart, in grape-like beauty shine!

XLVI.

NIGHT.

Day is passing, night is nigh;
    Hast thou, spirit, done thy best?
Quiet breadths of evening sky
    Tell thee there remains a rest.

Hast thou been of flesh the thrall?
    Now awhile at sunset free,
O, resolve, with morning's call,
    To assert thy liberty.

Dost thou breathe an anxious prayer
    Darkly, like a cloud of sighs?
Darkest clouds in glory share
    As they towards the zenith rise.

Through the sky, a temple dim,
    God is shining from the west;
And like shadowing cherubim,
    North and south his throne invest.

Rising through the temple's height,
    Prayers shall brighten as they meet
Streams of sweet and solemn light
    Flowing from that mercy-seat.

XLVII.

MIDNIGHT.

O HOLY ones, O watchers calm,
    While night anoints the earth with dew
In silent love, can any harm
    Befall us as we gaze on you?

Gazing on you, we honour Him
    Who sends to earth your welcome light
Across this dusky ocean dim
    Which circles round us every night.

Do spirits from your distant shore,
    Ye homes of bright tranquillity,
Sail sometimes, to see earth once more,
    Across this intervening sea?

Stand by us, when at solemn night,
    As once they did, for peace we yearn;
Whisper the secret, " All is right,"
    Then, blessing us, unseen return?

It must be so; and living ones,
    Unseen although they are so bright,
Shedding their life around like suns,
    Fill now the darkness with delight.

The starry air is full of bliss,—
    What evil can the soul befall?
The soul with friends surrounded is,
    And, lo! it loves the Lord of all.

XLVIII.

VICTORY.

Now have we met that we may ask
Recruited vigour for the task
    Of living as we would:
For we would live by that same word
Which all the honoured men have heard
    Who by their faith have stood.

By faith first vanquishing their fear,
They met each foe as he drew near,
    And still the victory won;
And often saved from deadly harm,
They sang anew the ancient psalm,
    "God is our shield and sun."

Through God alone can man be strong;
To comfort us He gave this song:
    "In Jesus Christ we stand;
Death held Him in his gloomy prison,
He broke the chains, and has arisen,
    To rule the deathless land."

His is the new and ancient word;
All wisdom man hath ever heard
    Hath been both his and He:
He is the very life of truth,
In Him it has eternal youth
    And certain victory.

An inner light, an inner calm
Have they who trust his champion arm,
   And hearing do his will:
For things are not as they appear;
In death is life, in trouble cheer,
   So faith is conqueror still.

Thus would we live; and therefore pray
For strength renewed, that we may say,
   Our life still upward tends:
If we who sing must sometimes sigh,
Yet life, beginning with a cry,
   In hallelujah ends.

XLIX.

DISCRETION.

Jesus, great friend of open speech
   Which wisdom prompts and wisdom leads,
True courage give, discretion teach,
   To every one for Thee who pleads.

Discreetly may we guard the truth
   From all dishonour to its fame;
And bold as with renewing youth,
   Indifferent be to foolish blame.

Discreetly may we guard our life
   From faults that its professions mock;
But boldly stand in error's strife,
   And meet proud contradiction's shock.

And ever at instruction's hour,
    O, may our spirit and our tongue
Work for the Church by mutual power,
    As for the body heart and lung.

Like bells, the loud alarm which sound,
    Yet send afar the cheerful news
Of peace achieved and victors crowned,
    O, may we all our voices use.

And O, oft fill us with the rush
    Of heavenly winds; for then shall burn
Tongues calmly bright, and all shall hush
    And towards the quiet glory turn.

L.

SHOWERS OF SONG.

As with sunny showers of song,
    Water now the new-sown grain;
Bright the blades must be and strong,
    Fullest ears we then may gain.

Scatter with the breeze of song,
    From the newly opened flowers,
Fragrance all our path along,
    Rich with salutary powers.

Thus the blessings of thy word
    Fully, Lord, ensure to those
Who have felt that, as they heard,
    Seeds were cast and blossoms rose.

Truths, by prompting us to sing,
    Better thy designs effect:
So, our grateful worshipping
    Thou, the Truth, wilt not reject.

LI.

EFFORT.

SEE the tide as advancing it breaks on the shingle,
    Then shines for a moment and ripples away;
Many waves in succession their efforts must mingle
    Before the bright waters will cover the bay.

See the effort of man as he onward advances,—
    The wave soon runs back or is broken in spray;
But the effort renews, and in spite of mischances
    To-morrow is still in advance of to-day.

Then, my soul, let no check to the truth be dismaying,
    Nor fear that thy rest will to thee be denied;
For the Church and each Christian, heaven's forces obeying,
    Shall float into harbour at height of the tide.

LII.

NEIGHBOURS.

O LORD, thou art not fickle;
    Our hope is not in vain;
The harvest for the sickle
    Will ripen yet again.

But though enough be given
    For all the world to eat,
Sin with thy love has striven
    Its bounty to defeat.

Were men to one another
    As kind as God to all,
Then no man on his brother
    For help would vainly call.

On none for idle wasting
    Would honest labour frown;
And none, to riches hasting,
    Would tread his neighbour down.

O, is there one in twenty
    With his own lot content,
Though God has bread and plenty
    To all the nations sent?

Till heart to heart is plighted
    In faith on heaven above,
Earth's harvests must be blighted
    For want of mutual love.

No man enough possesses
    Until he has to spare;
Possession no man blesses
    While self is all his care.

For blessings on our labour,
    O, then, in hope we pray,
When love unto our neighbour
    Is ripening every day.

LIII.

WHERE IS THY GOD?

Where is thy God, my soul?
    Is He within thy heart;
Or ruler of a distant realm
    In which thou hast no part?

Where is thy God, my soul?
    Only in stars and sun;
Or have the holy words of truth
    His light in every one?

Where is thy God, my soul?
    Confined to Scripture's page;
Or does his Spirit check and guide
    The spirit of each age?

O Ruler of the sky,
    Rule Thou within my heart;
O great Adorner of the world,
    Thy light of life impart.

Giver of holy words,
    Bestow thy holy power;
And aid me, whether work or thought
    Engage the varying hour.

In Thee have I my help,
    As all my fathers had;
I'll trust Thee when I'm sorrowful,
    And serve Thee when I'm glad.

LIV.

CITIZENSHIP.

FALLEN from ancestral glory,
    Shall we live unworthy days;
Dull to the inspiring story
    Of great Love's heroic praise?
Citizens of no mean city,
    If we bubbles idly chase

Scorn will dry the founts of pity,
    All men brand us with disgrace.

Christians! think what ye inherit,
    Read the archives of our State;
Jesus Christ is king by merit,
    O, be worthy and be great:
Foam-like, man with vain pretensions
    Dashing upwards sinks and dies:
Tree-like, saints to full dimensions
    Solidly and slowly rise.

We, of fathers learned, witty,
    And their lesser fame, are proud;
See the martyr, mystic city,
    Ages vest it like a cloud;
Cloudy Time with hues of glory
    Canopies its ancient fame;
Shall the lustre of its story
    But the darker make our shame?

Let us each some honoured father
    Emulate in new career;
Say not, "Who am I?" but rather,
    "Whose am I, that I should fear?
I am Christ's; and I will cherish
    Every dear ancestral name:
I am Christ's; I cannot perish,
    Partner of his power and fame."

Add a line unto the story,
    Add a name unto the roll,
Add a beam unto the glory,
    Add a part unto the whole :
Men, of ragstone and of rubble
    Palaces and churches build ;
Shall, of men, a Saviour's trouble
    Fail to rear what He hath willed ?

Let us each be humble, fervent,
    Bloom to heaven, but root in earth,
Show the royal eyes observant
    Homely, tender-hearted worth :
When the mingled crowd is sifted,
    Christ the tiniest grain will save ;
Locust-like let fears be drifted
    Down into oblivion's wave.

LV.

FAITH.

My faith, it is an oaken staff,
    The traveller's well-loved aid ;
My faith, it is a weapon stout,
    The soldier's trusty blade :
I'll travel on, and still be stirred
By silent thought or social word,
By all my perils undeterred,
    A soldier-pilgrim staid.

I have a Captain, and the heart
    Of every private man
Has drunk in valour from his eyes
    Since first the war began:
He is most merciful in fight,
And of his scars a single sight
The embers of our failing might
    Into a flame can fan.

I have a Guide, and in his steps
    When travellers have trod,
Whether beneath was flinty rock
    Or yielding grassy sod,
They cared not, but with force unspent,
Unmoved by pain, they onward went,
Unstayed by pleasures, still they bent
    Their zealous course to God.

My faith, it is an oaken staff,
    O, let me on it lean;
My faith, it is a trusty sword,
    May falsehood find it keen!
Thy Spirit, Lord, to me impart,
O, make me what Thou ever art,—
Of patient and courageous heart,
    As all true saints have been.

LVI.

PRAYER FOR THE HOLY SPIRIT.

Gracious Spirit, dwell with me,—
I myself would gracious be,
And with words that help and heal
Would thy life in mine reveal;
And with actions bold and meek
Would for Christ my Saviour speak.

Truthful Spirit, dwell with me,—
I myself would truthful be;
And with wisdom kind and clear
Let thy life in mine appear;
And with actions brotherly
Speak my Lord's sincerity.

Tender Spirit, dwell with me,—
I myself would tender be;
Shut my heart up like a flower
At temptation's darksome hour;
Open it when shines the sun,
And his love by fragrance own.

Silent Spirit, dwell with me,—
I myself would quiet be,
Quiet as the growing blade
Which through earth its way has made;
Silently, like morning light,
Putting mists and chills to flight.

Mighty Spirit, dwell with me,—
I myself would mighty be,
Mighty so as to prevail
Where unaided man must fail;
Ever by a mighty hope
Pressing on and bearing up.

Holy Spirit, dwell with me,—
I myself would holy be;
Separate from sin, I would
Choose and cherish all things good;
And whatever I can be
Give to Him who gave me Thee.

LVII.

MORNING.

O MORNING so bright,
   So sunny, so sweet,
Thou comest from God
   Our spirits to greet;
The weary heart rises,
   It cannot lie still;
Strange vigour surprises
   The care-fettered will.

How can we despair,
   Or brood on our wrong?
How can we be weak,
   When all things are strong?

The morning has smiled,
    And our hopes in the sun,
Like the feet of a child,
    Cannot move but they run.

With sorrow our ears
    Have oft been dismayed,
To sorrow our tears
    Some tribute have paid;
But tears from the sky
    Have been all wiped away;
This latest is bright
    As the earliest day.

Dark things that we know
    Now shall not distress;
All grievance and woe
    Our God will redress:
Bright things least expected
    We feel may be true,
Now joys have returned
    That we formerly knew.

O, be Thou our sun,
    Thou source of his flame,
Then joyful we run
    Who were tired and lame:
If love, in thy word,
    Like the morning arise,
Complaints are unheard,
    Incredulity dies.

No heart that desponds
    Desponding need stay;
Thou breakest our bonds
    At break of the day:
Our liberty won,
    And our heart full of praise,
This day of the sun
    Has the light of seven days.

LVIII.

SABBATH.

LORD, on thy returning day,
    From common labour freed,
We are come to sing and pray
    With felt returning need;
Come to seek our former rest,
Come to urge our old request.

Show us, Lord, the goal of life,
    And give us heart to run;
Breathe the peace that follows strife,
    Lest future work we shun:
Hearts that hasty time has grieved
Are by Sabbath calm relieved.

We would sing as in the rays
    Of mercy ever bright,
Which endureth, to thy praise,
    For ever thy delight:

Sing for happiness we know,
Or that we may happy grow.

We would pray as those who stand
    Their truest friend beside,
Whom He takes as by the hand
    Unto their God to guide:
By his power and for his sake
Fully us thy children make.

LIX.

WEEKDAY.

Lord, I on every day
With grateful heart would say,
" Thy truths are sure and beautiful;
How can my life grow dull?"

And when I eat and drink,
I joyfully would think,
That all Thou hast created good
May be a wise man's food.

And as I work and trade,
Pay others and am paid,
" Knowledge," I'll say, " we must not
    cease
To exchange, and so increase."

And when I hear the crowd
In busy traffic loud,
I'll cry, "How sweet would be the sound,
Were all but brothers found!"

And when my friends at night
Count my return delight,
I'll think how pleased my God will be
His child in heaven to see.

LX.

EVIL AS USURPER.

King of darkness, king of light,
Evil can but rule the night
As usurper, not by right,—
  Thine the true control.

In the busy crowded day
Thee we trust, to Thee we pray;
Else an entering shadow may
  Chill and blind our soul.

When the evening comes, we muse,
Till a brightening love bedews
So our hearts, they can but choose
  Now to offer praise:

For with sleep Thou canst not bless
Those whose wayward restlessness,
Through anxiety's excess,
      Troubles nights and days.

Now the slender starbeams are
Messengers from countries far,
Which on missions regular
      Come to give us hope,

That our fretting cares shall cease,
That the war shall end in peace,
And from limits blest release
      Yield desired scope.

LXI.

WALKING BY THE SEA.

I WALKED on sands beside the sea,
    And heard its ever-pulsing heart;
And mine was moved with sympathy,
    Desiring of such strength a part:
Thou restest not, nor needest rest,
    O sea; while I who love thee yet
Remain so weak, and at the best
    Am but a wish and a regret.

The moon with glory filled the air,
    With holy lustre very calm,
And all my thoughts in silence were
    Of fleeting good and frequent harm:

Yet happy with a heart so tired
    Beside the moonlit waves to stand;
I saw the good that I desired,
    Clear as my shadow on the sand.

I did not long to go to rest,
    I longed for rest to come to me,
And said, " Lord, O, that I were blest
    With strength and with serenity;
A heart as subject to thy will,
    And lighted with as calm a light,
As waves which now the harbour fill,
    And lift their crests so purely bright."

LXII.

CLOUDLESS NIGHT.

Lord of that undistracted realm
    Which cloudless night reveals,
Of every world Thou hast the helm,—
    What though the vessel reels?
If life is a tempestuous sea,
    Which winds imperious sway;
Though winds are mightier than we,
    Thou mightier art than they.

Like earth, O, does each quiet star
    A stormy passage urge,
And are we but away too far
    To hear the beating surge?

Thus through a distant valley's length
  Slow seems to glide the train,
And scarce is heard the throbbing strength
  Of the swift engine's strain.

One ruler is there of the seas,
  One pilot at the helm;
Our hearts are rising with the breeze,
  Fear cannot overwhelm:
O Jesus, Thou the ruler art,
  The captain kind and brave;
Sailing with Thee, our steadfast heart
  Defies the unsteady wave.

LXIII.

ONWARD AND UPWARD.

As we by successive stages
  Upward climb towards the sky,
Still a widening view engages
  An untired and wondering eye.

Though the mountain slopes are gusty,
  Torrents roar and chasms yawn,
Guide and staff alike are trusty,
  New fatigues are better borne.

Look! above us some are mounting,
  And below us some press on;
But we must not stop for counting
  Who has on this journey gone.

Mountain chains are but the bridges
   That a border district span,
Breathless from the topmost ridges
   Our new country we shall scan;

See its plains in plenty sweeping,
   See its bright and bowery homes;
There no hunger is, no weeping,
   There no grief, no spoiler, comes.

Ever in such mountain ranges
   Rugged difficulties stand;
He who crosses them exchanges
   Earth for the fair heavenly land.

LXIV.

REST.

O, REST a while, but only for a while;
   Life's business presses, and the time is short:
Ease may the weary of reward beguile;
   Let not the workman lose what he has wrought.

Rest for a while, if only for a while;
   The strong birds tire, and gladly seek their nest:
With quiet heart enjoy heaven's quiet smile;
   What strength has he who never takes his rest?

Rest for a while, though 'tis but for a while ;
  Home flies the bee, then soon re-quits the hive :
Rest on thy staff, walk then another mile ;
  Soon will the long, the final rest arrive.

O, rest a while, for rest is self return ;
  Leave the loud world, and visit thine own breast ;
The meaning of thy labours thou wilt learn,
  When thus at peace, with Jesus for thy guest.

LXV.

EARTH CLOTHED ANEW.

From each dark branchlet of the trees
  When starry buds begin to shine,
Their swelling light the watcher sees
  Soon break into a flowery sign
Of life no winters can subdue,
  And love that never can grow less ;
Which ancient plenty brings anew,
  With a forerunning loveliness.

The ever-unforsaken earth
  Is re-espoused in vernal hour,
And mid serenity and mirth
  Receives of wealth a starry dower :
Heaven plights his love to her anew,
  And clothes her in a wedding dress,
And will through changing months be true
  To this forerunning loveliness.

O heart, art thou again in flower,
    And does an inward force impel,
Itself impelled by heavenly power,
    Thy thought in happy hopes to swell?
Doth God again in covenant new
    Unite with thee thy life to bless?
Then let thy future work be true
    To such forerunning loveliness.

LXVI.

RENEWAL.

When the clouds so soft and tender
    Float upon the smiling blue,
Lord, our heart, that old offender,
    Asks that it may serve anew.

Winter now his sword is sheathing,
    And the warring winds are still,
Thou upon our hearts art breathing,
    And they lose constraint and chill.

All things happy seem and loving,
    All of tempers meek and sweet;
And the covered buds ungloving
    Seem with offered hand to greet.

Shall our hearts be dull and cheerless?
    O, forbid it mercy's powers;
Lord, we lowly will, yet fearless,
    Look Thee in the face like flowers.

When of days like these returning
  We with gentle sorrow think,
Days of holy hope and yearning,
  Lord, from facing Thee we shrink.

Yet, though former flowers were blighted,
  Wilt Thou present ones reject?
Let not offerings new be slighted;
  O, forgive our past neglect.

LXVII.

FOUNDATIONS.

  How firmly they stand,
  Who, piercing the sand,
Have reached and have built on the durable rock!
  The wind and the wave,
  However they rave,
Shall assault them in vain with impetuous shock.

  How sweet is the rest
  With which they are blest
Who the violent brunt of the storm have withstood,
  When silent and clear
  The heavens reappear
So eternally true and eternally good!

  But he that hath willed
  His dwelling to build
On the loose shifting sands of pretence and applause,

He hath not a home ;
For should the flood come,
He must fall by the stroke of reality's laws.

O, great is the fall,
When downward sink all,
Temples, houses, and palaces built on the sand ;
Though stately and gay,
More mighty than they
Is the tempest, which nothing but rock can withstand.

But if in life's course,
With merciful force,
Truth should come in a storm, and destroy thine abode ;
Thyself thou may'st save
From the threatening wave,
If with earnest repentance thou criest to God.

He gives thee anew
To choose for the true ;
Digging deep, found the house of obedient faith :
But why should the wise
Need terror's surprise
To teach them what wisdom convincingly saith ?

LXVIII.

SUSTENANCE.

O Thou, who by the meat and drink
    Which bounteous earth supplies
Enablest still the brain to think,
    And brightenest the eyes:

Who buildest up our fleshly frame,
    And dost that frame repair;
Changing, yet keeping it the same,
    With most mysterious care:

How can the mute unconscious bread
    Become the speaking tongue;
And nerves, through which our pleasures spread,
    And which by pain are wrung?

Can lifeless water help to form
    The living, leaping blood,
Whose gentle flow, in passion's storm
    Becomes a ruffled flood?

How much I know, yet know not how
    The thing I know can be:
The Lord of mysteries art Thou,—
    Lord, I believe in Thee.

The powers of common blood and flesh
　　My spirit foul and grieve :
O Lord, create my spirit fresh,
　　Then these new health receive.

On Christ, the meat and drink divine,
　　I feed my thoughts and heart ;
At each repast some acts are mine,
　　But thine the chiefest part.

Through Thee I stronger, better grow,
　　Old life for new exchange ;
Thy work divine by this I know,—
　　It blends the plain and strange.

LXIX.

SINGING.

In the fellowship of song
　　Let us worship happily ;
Evil spirits dark and strong
　　Fly before bright harmony.

Into hearts sweet music sinks
　　Like the rain-drops from the sky,
Which, when withering nature shrinks,
　　Fainting earth forbid to die.

Singing, lo, some truth of love,
 With an instantaneous light
Swift descending from above,
 Shines celestially bright;

Smites the fetters from our soul,
 Leaves the soul itself unscathed:
Soon we hear the thunder roll,
 And in balmier air are bathed.

Brightest truth's report we hear
 Echoing through the breadths of time;
And we hark with holy fear
 To the lingering sounds sublime.

Song, like storm, can shake the heart,
 All its feelings change and clear,
Bid the stagnant glooms depart
 That oppress life's atmosphere.

LXX.

FELLOWSHIP.

We come to the place of our rest,
 Each traveller comes with his friend;
A brotherly heart is the best,
 If heavenward our footsteps we bend:
How many the journey have gone!
 How various the tales that they tell!
But all who go patiently on
 Shall find at the end it is well.

We come to the temple of peace,
    As comrades we come from the war;
Our limbs from their armour release,
    To-morrow the sword we must draw.
We'll hear how the weak have prevailed,
    And think of the deeds they have done;
And then, when we next are assailed,
    Success may be easily won.

We come for the hour of repose,
    As labourers we come from our toil;
We'll think of the prosperous close,
    Nor rest let anxiety spoil:
We'll sit on the side of the hill,
    And look on the fields we have sown;
The ears are beginning to fill,
    The harvest will soon be our own.

LXXI.

REPOSE.

Our heart is like a little pool,
    Left by the ebbing sea,
Of crystal waters still and cool,
    When we rest musingly.

And see, what verdure exquisite,
    Within it hidden grows!
We never should have had the sight
    But for this brief repose.

And such a sight shall not be vain;
    These beauties they require
That we, though waves return again,
    Return when waves retire.

I'll oft return as to a book
    Written with heavenly art;
Intent beneath the surface look,
    And read in thee, my heart.

LXXII.

THE FOUNT OF LIFE.

SEE multitudes surrounding
    Life's fount admire its beauty;
But wisdom's word, how often heard
    When few have thought of duty:
It yields supplies abounding,
    And blest is the receiver;
Then shall we choose to praise the hues,
    Forgetting thirst and fever?

Once multitudes were gazing
    Upon one living centre,
The Son of Man, as He began
    On love's discourse to enter;
All the sweet words were praising,—
    Some wept as they were chidden;
But only few that Saviour knew,
    Who from the most was hidden.

Rise, fount of life, for ever;
    O Saviour, still be speaking;
For some reproved, by love are moved,
    And life's supply are seeking.
Truth's brilliance fading never
    Wins many an eye admiring;
And some around will still be found
    To quaff the draught inspiring.

LXXIII.

WINTER.

Slow is the fall to winter dark,
    As from the summer's height
The chillier days our progress mark
    And the still-lengthening night.

Slow are the steps by which we gain
    Our vernal liberty,
And long we drag the frosty chain
    That bound us heavily.

A happy progress, sure though slow,
    To bright and lengthening days,
Dost thou, O rescued spirit, know,
    And hast thou rendered praise?

Beware! another winter-tide
    May coldly shut thee in,
Through forces thou hast not defied
    Of slowly strengthening sin.

Let not thy summer ever fall
    Towards winter dark again;
Thy heart's sweet fields are covered all
    With heaven's swelling grain.

And golden light they every day
    Must drink in from the sun;
Then God will fetch his sheaves away
    When summer's course has run.

LXXIV.

WISDOM.

WISDOM coming from above
Fills for us the cup of love;
Drinking, let us upwards move
        Towards the seats of power.

Father, thine the royal throne;
All that hath thy power shown
Thou in love's design hast done,
        Done in wisdom's hour.

Let us through our Saviour wise,
By his loving spirit rise
To our Father in the skies;
        He is good and great.

O, were this but understood,—
To be great we must be good;
Learning then of Christ, we should
        Humbly serve and wait.

LXXV.

HEART OF CHRIST.

Heart of Christ, O cup most golden,
    Brimming with salvation's wine,
Million souls have been beholden
    Unto thee for life divine;
Thou art full of blood the purest,
Love the tenderest and surest:
Blood is life, and life is love;
O, what wine is there like love?

Heart of Christ, O cup most golden,
    Out of thee the martyrs drank,
Who for truth in cities olden
    Spake, nor from the torture shrank;
Saved they were from traitor's meanness,
Filled with joys of holy keenness:
Strong are those that drink of love;
O, what wine is there like love?

Heart of Christ, O cup most golden,
    To remotest place and time
Thou for labours wilt embolden
    Unpresuming but sublime:
Hearts are firm, though nerves be shaken,
When from thee new life is taken:
Truth recruits itself by love;
O, what wine is there like love?

Heart of Christ, O cup most golden,
    Taking of thy cordial blest,
Soon the sorrowful are folden
    In a gentle healthful rest:
Thou anxieties art easing,
Pains implacable appeasing:
Grief is comforted by love;
O, what wine is there like love?

Heart of Christ, O cup most golden,
    Liberty from thee we win;
We who drink, no more are holden
    By the shameful cords of sin;
Pledge of mercy's sure forgiving,
Powers for a holy living,—
These, thou cup of love, are thine;
Love, thou art the mightiest wine.

LXXVI.

DISCONTENT.

"Father, what portion of thy goods
    Falleth to me thy son?
Why are my brothers better off,
    With much where I have none?"

"My son, and hast thou known my love,
    And dost thou love me now?
Then many a far richer man
    Far poorer is than thou.

Thou hast thy Bible and thy bread;
    And waiting thou wilt see
The secret meaning of thy life,
    And all my care for thee.

Was not earth's most auspicious hour
    One darksome, sad, and wild?
When Crucifixion was the birth,
    Redemption was the child.

And by thine Elder Brother now
    I am redeeming thee;
He gives thee, that thou mayst be rich,
    To feel thy poverty.

He gives thee, that thou mayst be kind,
    To grieve at cold neglect;
He gives thee, that thou mayst be wise,
    To feel thine own defect.

He gives thee, that celestial joy
    Thy common hours may bless,
To feel in all the shows of earth
    Essential nothingness.

One loving Brother, then, thou hast,
    Who makes his wealth thine own:
He goodness is; and what are goods
    If God remain unknown?"

LXXVII.

SUCCESS.

O God, our spirits unassisted
    Must unsuccessful be ;
Who ever hath the world resisted
    Except by help from Thee ?
But saved by a divine alliance
    From terrors of defeat,
Unvauntingly, yet with defiance,
    One man the world may meet.

Disciples see their Master bleeding
    Upon the dreadful cross ;
Hopeless of better days succeeding,
    They mourn the battle's loss :
But at this hour of their bewailing,
    While sin on sorrow rails,
'Tis man who triumphs that is failing,
    'Tis Christ who dies prevails.

Though evil hearts together leaguing
    May do the righteous wrong ;
And cruel craft with force intriguing
    Feel confidently strong;
We know, if but the Saviour's story
    With heart of faith we read,
That God through sufferings unto glory
    Salvation's sons will lead.

Say not, O soul, thou art defeated,
    Because thou art distrest;
If thou of better things art cheated,
    Thou canst not be of best:
Thy heaviest sighs with swift ascending
    Plead, and thy God attends;
And soon, the clouded heavens rending
    In comfort's beam descends.

My soul is for a crown aspiring,
    The crown of righteousness;
My soul is for the truth inquiring,—
    For God, and nothing less:
Sin, sorrow, and the dark conspiring,
    Assault me, and I bleed;
Tired am I, but through love untiring
    I know I shall succeed.

LXXVIII.

SACRED HAPPINESS.

Spirit of sacred happiness,
    Who makest energy delight,
    And love to be in weakness might;
Now with enlivening impulse bless,
Now re-confirm our steadfastness,
    And make us vigorous and bright.

Blessed be Thou, O Heart supreme,
    Sweet charity's unfailing well,
    Whose bounty all the countries tell;

Drinking of Thee, with sunny gleam
Forth-leaping into action's stream,
    Our heart's replenished fountains swell.

Both work and sport Thou hallowest,
    Canst blissful make the busiest days,
    And woes that else benumb and craze
By Thee to finer joys are blest,
And hearts, of deeper power possest,
    With grateful tears thy wisdom praise.

Spirit of bliss and sanctity,
    Who art invincible in good,
    Who hate and mockery hast withstood
In every age; how coward we,
How selfish, restless, till by Thee
    Inspired to do the thing we would!

By unremorseful joys, O, woo
    Our hearts to holy efforts still;
    Now with young life volition fill;
For child-like, we are god-like too,—
Likest our Father when we do
    With filial love and haste his will.

LXXIX.
WORK.

My work appointed I have done,
I who the work in doubt begun;
In mercy, Lord, accept from me
All that appointed was by Thee.

Never would I commence a task
But I thy will would know or ask:
But often I present to Thee
A good work done too wilfully.

The wise must heavenly service do
In heavenly mode and measure too;
Else their appointed tasks may be
Done rather to themselves than Thee.

How oft we persevere in pride
With work that should be laid aside!
How oft thy choicer works postpone
For others that are more our own!

Leave me not, Lord, and I will be
A better servant unto Thee;
And what I have in zeal begun
Shall with discretion too be done.

And what I do with my delight,
And what I do with all my might,
Nor joy nor ardour shall pervert,
To cause my weakness and my hurt.

My words are of my heart: O, hear,
And give me a love-tempered fear;
Then work and working both shall be
Appointed and approved by Thee.

LXXX.

PROTECTION.

Since penalties so fearful
    Thou dost to sin award,
How can our heart be cheerful,
    How can we love Thee, Lord?
Because Thou still art gracious,
    Lord, even in thine ire,—
Round blissful heaven spacious
    It is protective fire.

Fear makes our souls the fitter
    To prize thy love and Thee;
For if the curse be bitter,
    Sweet must the blessing be:
O, sweet to hear Thee saying,
    "Peace, heart, be ever still;"
O, sweet the full obeying
    Of thine eternal will.

To Thee our heart is crying
    Amid deceiving sin,
And worldly fears defying
    The faith that rules within:
We from estranging error
    Our love to Thee would guard;
To us the chiefest terror
    Is lest we leave Thee, Lord.

Be fear to us a measure
    For valuing our hope;
And teach how great our treasure,
    How great salvation's scope;
How great the love unsparing
    Of Him who for us died;
How great the mercy caring
    New succours to provide.

O, may we know Thee zealous
    To save us from our pain;
But ever wisely jealous
    Lest sin advantage gain:
In smiting what Thou hatest,
    Such love is in thy wrath,
That all which Thou createst
    The surer glory hath.

LXXXI.

JERUSALEM.

See, bannered armies hem
    The favoured city round;
Vain are thy towers, Jerusalem;
    False art thou found:
With hills divinely girt
    And massive walls of stone,
Impregnable to others' hurt,
    Lost by thine own.

Thy Temple, like a gem,
    Adorns thee, faithless bride;
Thy God, O fair Jerusalem,
    Hath left thy side:
Ah, happy once and blest,
    A golden-feathered dove,
When, like the jewel on thy breast,
    Shone forth thy love.

A fruitless, fallen stem,
    Low on the miry earth
Lies beautiful Jerusalem,
    Spoiled of her worth;
Fire through her branches runs,—
    Consume her! she hath sinned;
Like ashes now her scattered sons
    Fly on the wind.

My soul, lament for them;
    Learn from this fatal fall;
For of a new Jerusalem
    Sons are we all:
Round us are mightier towers,
    A brighter heaven above:
O, be the Lord's, as He is ours,
    In faithful love.

LXXXII.

OLD AND NEW.

Breathe on us for the passing day
    The powers of ancient story;
Then we with joyful heart shall say,
    "Though Wisdom's head be hoary,
His heart is fresh, undimmed his eyes;
And in the old we must be wise,
    If we would win new glory."

New is the world at every hour,
    New runners find new races;
New is the spirit's prompting power,
    New hearts obtain new graces:
But old and new are faith and love,
And the great thought, all thoughts above,
    First things and last embraces.

How came it, men of faith, to pass
    That ye were mighty-handed?
How brake ye down the gates of brass
    When few of ye were banded?
It was that through your open soul
God like a tide did onward roll,
    And left no vessel stranded.

How was it, lovers of your kind,
    Though ye were mocked and hated,
That ye with clear and patient mind
    Truth's holy doctrine stated?

In God, as in an ark, ye kept;
Around, and not above you, swept
   The flood till it abated.

O Father of all mighty men,
   A river-fount unsealing
In our dry hearts, O, let us then
   See Christ in full revealing;
Touched by the sceptre of his cross,
With knightly scorn of shame and loss,
   We shall arise from kneeling.

The rivers never backward run
   That for the sea are yearning,
And never is the mid-day sun
   Found on his course returning:
By gathering force, and onward stress,
And strengthening beams, all doubt repress,
   My soul, thyself concerning.

LXXXIII.

WEAK THOUGH SINCERE.

WEAK we are, although sincere;
   But in our sincerity
Pleading weakness, we are here
   To obtain a hope from Thee,
     That we never
   Shall our own confusion see.

Often ready is our heart,
    Longing for an early rest,
From its labours to depart
    While of little yet possest:
      O, may patience
    Faith confirm, and love attest!

Pleasures sweet and praises bright,—
    These the spirit may betray:
O, how suddenly we might
    Fail on some unguarded day,
      And by yielding
    Cast the hope of years away!

Happy for us is the hour
    When from sinning we recoil;
Happy when the inward power
    Quickens at the view of toil:
      But the happiest
    Sad surprises may despoil.

For desires that secretly
    Gain dominion in the breast,
When comes opportunity
    From the will its mastery wrest;
      Proving evil
    Known and mourned is not supprest.

Thou who wast in all behaviour
    Ever equal, free from sin,

Be to us a daily Saviour;
    Over secret evil win
        Secret conquest:
Reign without, because within.

LXXXIV.

CONTRASTS.

LORD, how wonderful is man
    In frailty and in force;
Eagle-like he upward can
    Fly to the sacred source
Of his light and of his love;
    But ah, how quickly is he found,
Stone-like, falling from above,
    Or fluttering on the ground!

Should our hearts, that in the sun
    On eagles' wings can move,
When the storms have but begun
    As weak as insects prove?
Hearts that have seemed firm as towers,—
    O, high in aim, in strength how brief!—
Fly before the windy showers,
    Like an autumnal leaf?

Wings must often shrink and fail
    Until the heart be right;
Faith alone can face the gale
    With an unflagging might;

Stormy clouds it pierces through,
    For bold and patient are its wings;
Reaching heavens bright and blue,
    It still ascends and sings.

Man is like a flame of fire,
    That to a spark may die,
Yet recovering re-aspire
    In streams towards the sky.
What though broken be his wing,
    In Thee, O Lord, his help is found;
From new hearts new pinions spring,
    And bear us from the ground.

LXXXV.

BRIGHTNESS.

How often on a morning bright,
    Lord, whom we cannot see,
Because Thou dwellest in the light,
    We feel we are with Thee!

The sky is then so beautiful,
    It keenly brings to mind
Our many wishes dutiful,
    Thy many bounties kind.

And pleasure seeks to make us wise,
    Intenser for the pain
With which these memories arise
    Of wishes that were vain:

Of wishes that have hastened toward
    Thy work, yet would not stay;
Like him who ran to seek the Lord,
    Yet sorrowing went away.

To be invited we were glad,
    Yet glad to be excused;
Occasion's hour a welcome had,
    And yet it passed unused.

But God in light has come again,
    And comforts though He grieves;
For happiness is born of pain
    To him who but believes.

Through tangled thoughts thy mercy dear
    Shines with a richer grace;
As skies are seen more sweetly clear
    Through boughs that interlace.

LXXXVI.

SHADOWS.

SHADOWS now are darker growing,
    But the friendly planet bright
Momently is overflowing
    With a fuller, clearer light:
        See how mildly
    Every star confronts the night.

Say'st thou, "Times are darker growing?"
   In the darkness gather might;
To the grateful traveller showing
   God hath set thee for a light:
     Mildly constant
   Shine, and help to rule the night.

O, be steadier in thy duty;
   O, be brighter in thy zeal;
O, be holier in thy beauty,
   When the earth most needs to feel
     What the Christian
   Can perform to bless and heal.

LXXXVII.

SPIRIT OF BEAUTY.

SPIRIT of beauty! thy presence confessing,
   God can we see in a sparkle of ore;
Flowers and shells to our heart are expressing
   Love like its own, but transcendently more.

Spirit of beauty! each bough in its bending,
   Skies in their curve, and the sea in its swell,
Streams as they wind, hills and plains in their blending,
   All, in our own, of God's happiness tell.

Spirit of beauty! thou soul of our Maker,
    Suddenly shown in a gleam or a tint;
O, be each heart of thy joy a partaker;
    Love, and its store, are alike without stint.

Spirit of beauty! thou teachest us sweetly;
    Prophets and psalmists yield holy delight:
Show us our Lord, and we then shall completely
    Know thee as gentle, omnipotent might.

Spirit of beauty! our offering we render,
    Thee in thy skyey dominion we praise;
Lark-like we rise to the shadowless splendour,
    Pouring out song as the sun pours his rays.

LXXXVIII.

QUIET.

As to a quiet valley
    The lowly-hearted come,
And there recruit and rally
    While threatening winds are dumb:
Care cried, their doubt abetting,
    "Why any more believe?
The world is harsh and fretting,
    For sin you vainly grieve."

But now, at ease reclining,
    Intent they look above,

And see the lucid shining
    Of pure primeval love;
The strength of one day's quiet,
    And one day's full repast
On truth's celestial diet,
    For all the week will last.

With new and tender grieving
    Their doubts they so lament,
That soon all unbelieving
    Is lost in sweet content:
Through griefs a joy is shining,
    As light shines through a tear;
Like dews with life combining,
    They shine and disappear.

The cry is now for vigour
    Onwards in faith to press,
Warm-hearted, through the rigour
    Of the cold wilderness:
O Lord, we are not hardened,
    Thy life refills our heart;
O, let the doubt be pardoned
    That Thou the pardoner art.

O Saviour, thy perfection
    For ours in heaven pleads;
Thoughts of thy resurrection,
    They are as fiery steeds,

Which now our hearts are raising,
  Like chariots bright with love;
Our voice thy bounty praising,
  As we are borne above.

We who in valleys quiet,
  So holy, hushed, and warm,
While unconfused by riot,
  Unbuffeted by storm,
Are towards the land ascending
  Whence was our Saviour's birth,
To-morrow must be wending
  The way He trod on earth.

LXXXIX.

BEFORE SERMON.

Be thy word with power fraught,
  Many hearts in many ways
Blessing with new love and thought
  To religion's added praise.

Be it for the rash restraint,
  Ardour for the dull and cold;
Be it comfort for the faint,
  Be it counsel for the bold.

Be it for the tempest-worn
  Haven for a quiet stay;
May it, like the wakening horn,
  Summon cheerful souls away.

May some saddened hearts arise,
    And be blossoms in the light;
Some, like stars in clearing skies,
    Trembling be, yet very bright.

As in whisper or in shout,
    Calming, rousing, Lord, be heard;
Such thy voice, that even doubt
    Cries "'Tis He," and "'Tis his word."

XC.

GOD'S ANSWERS.

OFT when of God we ask
    For fuller, happier life,
He sets us some new task
    Involving care and strife:
Is this the boon for which we sought?
Has prayer new trouble on us brought?

This is indeed the boon,
    Though strange to us it seems;
We pierce the rock, and soon
    The blessing on us streams;
For when we are the most athirst,
Then the clear waters on us burst.

We toil as in a field,
    Wherein, to us unknown,

A treasure lies concealed,
    Which may be all our own :
And shall we of the toil complain
That speedily will bring such gain?

We dig the wells of life,
    And God the waters gives;
We win our way by strife,
    Then He within us lives;
And only war could make us meet
For peace so sacred and so sweet.

XCI.

GLIMPSES.

LIKE one who blind sits rushes weaving,
    And listens to a constant stream,
Feels the warm sun, but still is grieving
    Because he sees no sunny gleam;
So darkly I my life was spending,
    And all my work seemed mean and frail;
Time's sound with love's sweet warmth was blending,
    But, ah, I wore a heavy veil.

Lo, now I see; but when I'm musing,
    With God I seem, and yet apart;
And like a tear the eye suffusing,
    So swells a sorrow in my heart:

A pain is mingling with my pleasure,
    My joy is neither full nor pure,
My light has clouds in over-measure,
    My glimpse of God will not endure.

And when the light renews its shining,
    And strengthens me to wait awhile,
Still do I thirst, though not repining,—
    I crave a word, a look, a smile.
Yet, heart! from hope be parted never;
    Behold, thou seest, who blind hast been;
Thy thirst shall be appeased for ever,—
    Soon shalt thou see as thou art seen.

XCII.

UNBELIEF FORBIDDEN.

MOUNTAINS by the darkness hidden
    Are as real as in the day;
Be, then, unbelief forbidden
    In a dreary hour to say,
"God hath left us, God hath left us;
    O, why hath He gone away?"

When He folds the cloud about Him,
    Firm within it stands his throne;
Wherefore should his children doubt Him,
    Those to whom his love is known?
God is with us, God is with us;
    We are never left alone.

Travellers at night, by fleeing,
    Cannot run into the day:
God can lead the blind and seeing;
    On Him wait, and for Him stay:
Be not fearful, be not fearful;
    They who cannot sing can pray.

O, the bright and vast creation
    Can be terrible and stern,
From its stroke be no salvation,
    Though on every side we turn:
Lord of nature, Lord of nature,
    Then to Thee our spirits yearn.

Calm and blest is our composure
    When the secret is possest,
That our God in full disclosure
    Hath to us his heart exprest;
Thou, O Saviour, Thou, O Saviour,
    Hast been given to give us rest.

Space and time, O Lord, that show Thee
    Oft in power veiling good,
Are too vast for us to know Thee
    As our trembling spirits would;
But in Jesus, yes, in Jesus,
    Father, Thou art understood.

XCIII.

SILENCE.

In silence mighty things are wrought,—
Silently builded, thought on thought,
    Truth's temple greets the sky;
And like a citadel with towers,
The soul with her subservient powers
    Is strengthened silently.

Soundless as chariots on the snow
The saplings of the forest grow
    To trees of mighty girth;
Each nightly star in silence burns,
And every day in silence turns
    The axle of the earth.

The silent frost with mighty hand
Fetters the rivers and the land
    With universal chain;
And smitten by the silent sun,
The chain is loosed, the rivers run,
    The lands are free again.

O Source unseen of life and light,
Thy secrecy of silent might
    If we in bondage know,
Our hearts, like seeds beneath the ground,
By silent force of life unbound,
    Move upwards from below.

And if our hearts well rooted be,
Their love, like sap within the tree,
   With silent quickening moves;
Enlarged and liberated powers,
More light and balmier warmth are ours,
   And God his presence proves.

O Saviour, who, that silence keeps,
But sometimes at the story weeps
   Of all that he has known?
That we are what we are, how strange!
How gradual the silent change
   By which our souls have grown!

XCIV.

EXPECTATION.

ALL faded is the glowing light
   That once from heaven shone,
When startled shepherds in the night
   The angels came upon.

O, shine again, ye angel host,
   And say that He is near;
Though but a simple few at most
   Believe He will appear.

Ye heavens, that have been growing dark,
   Now also are ye dumb;
When shall the listeners say, "Hark,
   They're singing—He will come?"

Lord, come again, O, come again,
    Come even as Thou wilt;
But not anew to suffer pain,
    And strive with human guilt.

O, come again, Thou mighty King,
    Let earth thy glory see;
And let us hear the angels sing,
    "He comes with victory."

XCV.

PROGRESS.

BEHOLD, how mighty truth,
    From a first glimmer pale,
With gradual ray extends its sway,
    Through heaven to prevail:
Sing ye praises, O, sing praises;
    For truth can never fail.

Behold, how mighty love,
    That from a firstling flower,
By gradual heats, reveals its sweets,
    Gains universal power:
Sing ye praises, O, sing praises;
    And hail love's prospering hour.

The God of truth and love,
    The ancient friend of man,
Makes every age an onward stage,
    And has since time began:

Sing ye praises, O, sing praises ;
   God has a glorious plan.

Though wisdom, like a cloud,
   Is undefined when bright,
We will not stay, but haste away,
   And keep the cloud in sight :
Sing ye praises, O, sing praises ;
   'Tis never wholly night.

Lo, from the cloud a shape
   Looks forth our souls to greet,—
The Lord of grace, I see his face,
   And run with bounding feet :
Sing ye praises, O, sing praises ;
   Sing grateful praises sweet.

If once from out the light
   His smile on us has shone,
Again the cloud his face may shroud,
   Yet boldly we'll go on :
Sing ye praises, O, sing praises ;
   The dusk will soon be gone.

Christ is our guide, our guard,
   On us no foes can prey ;
Nor can we roam, for to our home
   He leads us night and day :
Sing ye praises, O, sing praises,
   While on your homeward way.

XCVI.

INCONSTANCY.

O, were I ever what I am sometimes,
    And never more what I sometimes have been!
For oft my spirit, singing as it climbs,
    Can make of winter bleak a summer green:
And yet sometimes, and in the sunniest weather,
My work and I have fallen out together.

Now, earth seems drossy, heaven the land of gold;
    Anon, heaven fabulous, substantial earth;
And sometimes in my God I can be bold,
    And say, "What hopes are mine in right of birth!"
And yet sometimes at former faith I wonder,
And fears I once defied I now sink under.

Lord, rid me of this natural waywardness,
    Unworthy one who is a child of thine;
Calm let me be when rudest winds distress,
    Nor lose occasion if the day be fine;
But, faithful to the light of sacred reason,
One heart be mine in every changing season.

XCVII.

THE COMING SUMMER.

The soul's sweet summer is not here,
    But only breaths and flowers;
Its open glory will appear,
    But secret now its powers.

Life here is like spring's fickle time,
    Alternate blight and balm;
But heaven will be our summer's prime,
    One bright unending calm.

O, glad we are, yet scarce begun
    Our day of happiness;
The light of an unrisen sun
    Is all that we possess.

The joy with which our souls are blest,
    How silent and how pure!
But joy is twilight at the best,
    Although of sunrise sure.

Spirit of Christ, through Thee we oft
    The coming summer feel;
Thou canst, in hallowing glory soft,
    A budding world reveal.

Our hearts with an increasing glow
    Of morning hope, O, fill;
Christ's coming day we then shall know
    By joys devout and still.

XCVIII.

FREEDOM.

The chrysalis in crannies lies,
    Content awhile to be obscure ;
    But higher happiness is sure
When forth on quivering wings he flies.

He from his hovel dark shall come,
    Of wisdom's secret giving proof ;
    And summer skies shall be the roof
That spans his new palatial home.

Formed in thine earthly tenement,
    O man of earth, when thou shalt die,
    A heavenly self shall upwards fly,
If thou art wise : then be content.

Believe in God, and soon shalt thou,
    Darkly maturing in thy prison,
    Follow the good, who, having risen,
Enjoy resplendent freedom now.

XCIX.

AUTUMN.

The sere leaf flickers down
    O'er gardens in decay ;
For leafy robe and flowery crown
    Must both be put away :

The summer says farewell,
  With hushed and tender tone:
Fear not, the buds again will swell,
  The blossoms be thine own.

The incense in the smoke,
  While offerings burnt away,
Of God's abiding favour spoke;
  So now in this decay:
The thoughts of holy rest,
  While summers disappear,
Diffuse around the fragrance blest
  Of God's eternal year.

In what a tender light
  Do summers fade and die,
As if their spirit took its flight
  In tranquil ecstasy!
I will not mourn the signs
  Of death so sweetly calm;
Immortal hope, that round me shines,
  Brings every grief a balm.

I'll blossom and bear fruit
  While glowing summers last;
And still the murmurings confute
  That say, "Thy joys are past."
My joy is yet to come;
  For through the sombre gates
Of dark decay we reach the home
  Where life undying waits.

C.

DEPARTURE.

Departing in peace,
With gentle release,
The dream-weary soul from its slumbers is freed;
And hearing heaven's lays,
It cries in amaze,
"Ah, Lord, and now am I in heaven indeed?

How can I believe
I no more shall grieve,—
For ever awake from my dream-burdened sleep?
Too full my delight,
The morning too bright:
Ah, Lord, I'm so happy, permit me to weep.

What light and what balm!
What thrill, yet what calm!
My heart feels at once like a bridegroom and bride
Lo, coming on me
Thy likeness I see:
Ah, Lord, 'tis enough,—I am now satisfied."

CI.

PATIENCE.

Most high and patient God,
When I a lonely man
Sit silent in my narrow place,
And try the world to scan,

How mighty Evil seems!
    How frail the Truth!
And, O, I sorrow for the dreams
    That blest my youth.

I hear a coming throng,
    Some great one passes by;
And brazen music clangs aloud
    His iron victory;
So great the general joy,
    I too feel glad:
Then, " 'Tis but vanity!" I say,
    And so am sad.

And yet, most humble God,
    I crave magnificence;
O, purest meekness for my soul,
    But splendour for my sense:
I want the heavenly King
    To come in state;
I want to see, and feel, and sing
    The good are great:

To see, as in my dreams,
    Huge evil cower and end;
And hear huzzas on every side
    With hallelujahs blend;
The whispered truth to hear
    Proclaimed aloud;
And see mankind a holy church
    And happy crowd.

CII.

REAPING.

When happy Christian hope began,
    This was its crown and sum,
That He who came as Son of man
    As Son of God would come;
For He, the Sower, must return
    His harvest-field to reap,
The wheat to garner, and to burn
    Of tares the wasteful heap.

Then Truth the sufferer shall rejoice,
    And Truth dishonoured shine;
And Truth denied be in a voice
    Of thunder hailed divine;
And Truth the patient worker rest,
    Abundant wealth his own;
And Truth the warrior be blest
    With victory and a throne.

He came to save, and angel-songs
    But introduced his grief;
He comes to judge, and wailing throngs
    But tell of earth's relief:
Let folly and let falsehood fear,
    But all the nations sing;
The Truth Himself at last is here,
    Our own majestic King.

We saw Him, but we did not know
    That Goodness was our God;
And Justice with no sword to show
    Beneath our feet we trod:
And though a light from virtue streams
    That makes all heaven glad,
A virtue without golden beams
    To us no beauty had.

Yet for us on the cross He crossed
    The river dark and deep,
Though angrily the black waves tossed,
    The champion back to keep;
And conquering, He to earth again
    As King of life shall come;
And mightily in joy shall reign,
    Of hope the crown and sum.

CIII.

DIVINE FIRE.

With feet of burning brass,
    When times are dark as night,
Thou through the world dost pass,
    Consuming in our sight
Dry trees and withering grass,
    With dreadful, happy light.

O Thou consuming fire,
    Why should I fear thy flame,

Who purpose and desire
    To burn what Thou shalt blame,
Ill weeds, and every brier
    Of folly and of shame?

With shining beams that smite
    The chains of darkness through,
Thou smilest in the height,
    And all things smile anew;
Thy heat, in subtle might,
    Works with the gentle dew.

O Thou creating fire,
    I feel thy warmth benign;
My hopes a flowering spire
    Arise, unfold, and shine;
And fruits that I desire
    Shall soon be mine and Thine.

CIV.

ANOTHER DAY.

ANOTHER day may bring another mind,
    A mind to learn, when there is none to teach;
To follow, when no leader we can find;
    To enjoy, when good is now beyond our reach:

A better mind, but not a better time,
    A mind to will, but not a time to do
What had been done, if we in life's bright prime,
    When God was ready, had been ready too.

But what the better for his better mind
    Were changing man, and God not still the same?
When guide and light and joy we cannot find,
    Unchanging love has sent us useful shame.

This other mind may bring another day,
    For days are given as man for days prepares;
Though many days of grace have passed away,
    The grace that gave them still the trifler spares;

And saddens times while Time itself may last,
    That unwise man may come to better thought,
Accept his future, and renounce his past,
    And be by sorrow into goodness brought.

CV.

THE CHILD. *Isa.* ix. 6.

THE world was dark with care and woe,
    With brawl and pleasure wild,
When in the midst, his love to show,
    God set a child.

The sages frowned, their beards they shook,
    For pride their heart beguiled;
They said, each looking on his book,
    "We want no child."

The merchants turned towards their scales,
　　Around their wealth lay piled;
Said they, "'Tis gold alone prevails;
　　We want no child."

The soldiers rose in noisy sport,
　　Disdainfully they smiled,
And said, "Can babes the shield support?
　　We want no child."

The merry sinners laughed or blushed,
　　Alas, and some reviled;
All cried, as to the dance they rushed,
　　"We want no child."

The old, the afflicted, and the poor,
　　With voices harsh or mild,
Said, "Hope to us returns no more;
　　We want no child."

And men of grave and moral word,
　　With consciences defiled,
Said, "Let the old truth still be heard;
　　We want no child."

Then said the Lord, "O world of care
　　So blinded and beguiled,
Thou must become for thy repair
　　A holy child.

And unto thee a Son is born,
    Thy second hope has smiled;
Thou mayst, though sin and trouble worn,
    Be made a child."

CVI.

THE SON OF THE HIGHEST. Luke i. 32.

O LITTLE one who art so great,
    To-day there would be weeping skies;
For holy heaven foresees the hate
    Against Thee that on earth will rise;
Were not the holy heaven sure
That love will work of hate the cure.

A heart the gladdest and the best
    Thou hast, thy Father's babe and ours;
Smile, little one, in happy rest,
    There wait Thee dark tumultuous hours;
I see them, O, I see them near,
And almost wish thou wert not here.

I know Thee, Jesus, who Thou art;
    But what have we to do with Thee,
That Thou shouldst choose the bitterest part,
    And sink Thyself in misery?
Sorrows thy love will steep Thee in,
But sorrows love for Thee will win.

Rest, nursling, in thine innocence;
    King Herod's dagger cannot slay;
To darker death Thou goest hence,
    Toiling along a narrow way,
Which ever leads from bad to worse,
All thorny with an ancient curse.

A curse! O mother, dost thou hear
    What must befall thy little son?
Smile, baby, at thy mother's tear,
    The blessing by the curse is won;
Purer than snow will be our gains,
By horror of his crimson stains.

CVII.

THE GOOD NEWS.

A THOUSAND years have come and gone,
    And near a thousand more,
Since happier light from heaven shone
    Than ever shone before;
And in the hearts of old and young
    A joy most joyful stirred,
That sent such news from tongue to tongue
    As ears had never heard.

Then angels on their starry way
    Felt bliss unfelt before,
For news that men should be as they
    To darkened earth they bore;

So toiling men and spirits bright
    A first communion had,
And in meek mercy's rising light
    Were each exceeding glad.

And we are glad, and we will sing,
    As in the days of yore;
Come all, and hearts made ready bring
    To welcome back once more
The day when first on wintry earth
    A summer change began,
And dawning in a lowly birth
    Uprose the Light of man.

For trouble such as men must bear
    From childhood to fourscore,
He shared with us, that we might share
    His joy for evermore;
And twice a thousand years of grief,
    Of conflict and of sin,
May tell how large the harvest-sheaf
    His patient love shall win.

CVIII.

ANNI DOMINI.

O WONDROUS, weary years,
    That since the Saviour came,
Roughened with strife and dark with tears,
    Have borne his name!

Years of the Lord are these,
　　But of a Lord away;
Therefore temptation and the cross
　　Have had the sway.

When shall the mystery end,
　　And storms disperse the gloom,
That earth may see the sun, and like
　　A garden bloom?

Then wondrous, happy years,
　　From that triumphant hour,
Too calm for strife, too bright for tears,
　　Shall speak his power.

CIX.

THE NEW YEAR.

AGAIN from mid-winter
　　Comes forth the new year;
Heir to strifes and to troubles,
　　But born without fear:
Through the eyes of this infant
　　The Ancient of Days
Looks with beams of prediction,
　　To scatter dismays.

He, the mighty King, ruleth,
　　Immovably calm;
No storms can his kingdom
　　By any means harm;

And his age-blazoned banner
  Still shines on the wind,
To rally the legions
  That fight for mankind.

Forth we steam through the tempest
  In confidence bold;
Faith's unbreakable cable
  Hope's anchor will hold:
Forth we march to the battle
  With this in our mind,
That men may be conquered,
  But never mankind.

If mid clouds tempest-laden
  Our new morning breaks,
And the strong-rooted nations
  A rising wind shakes,
From behind terror's tokens,
  Assuringly through,
There shines on for ever
  The pitying blue.

But, O, coming Saviour,
  When speak'st Thou the word,
" Be sheathed, sword of nations;
  Shine, sword of the Lord?"
When shall war, the blind Samson,
  Thy victory know,
And in a last carnage
  Himself overthrow?

O, come, mighty Jesus,
    Earth calls to Thee, come!
The rainbow is brightest
    When darkest the gloom;
In the clouds red and murky
    Thy promise we see,
And the loud-pealing thunders
    Are trumpets of Thee.

All other thrones broken,
    When wilt Thou build one
As firm as the mountains,
    As bright as the sun?
When, with last desolations
    Earth's weedage consume,
That in unbeheld beauty
    Thine Eden may bloom?

That day for advancing,
    New year! thou art sent;
Thy strifes shall but hasten
    Love's mighty event;
When the long-estranged kindreds
    In one blood made nigh,
The hymn, "Christ is reigning,"
    Shall swell to the sky.

CX.

SIN OVERCOME.

BENEATH the darkest, basest will
    Of human hate and pride,
Thou dost, with overcoming skill,
    A deeper purpose hide;
Men can but lift the spear to kill,
    That through the wound may pour
Mercies, the thirsty world to fill,
    And flow for evermore.

When down they tear the Tree of Life,
    And burn it like a weed,
Their wrath is but a priestly knife,
    Thy Love the lamb indeed.
With living seeds all winds are rife,
    Though fire the green tree burns;
And the pale Victim, in the strife,
    Eternal priesthood earns.

Thus, through the follies we have done,
    Thou dost our good pursue;
Nor evil that we have begun
    Wilt let us finish too;
But endest all things by thy Son,
    Who with all sins has striven,
That through forgiveness we may shun
    The sins Thou hast forgiven.

CXI.

PETER'S TEARS.

What tears are these that flow so fast?
    The cock hath crowed for coming dawn,
Twice hath he crowed; the night is past;
    With new day let new hope be born.

It was the Lord at cock-crow came;
    Like Moses' rod, with double stroke,
A voice smote Simon in his shame;
    Christ looked,—the strong man's heart was broke.

He weeps, and bitter are his tears,
    As bitter as his words were base,
As urgent as the sudden fears
    Which even love refused to face.

O, love so false and yet so true,
    O, love so eager yet so weak,
In these sad waters born anew
    Thy tongue shall yet in triumph speak.

Thou livest, and the boaster dies,
    Dies with the night that wrought his shame;
Thou livest, and these tears baptise—
    Simon, now Peter is thy name.

A rock, upon Himself the Rock
    Christ places thee this awful day;
Him waves assault with direful shock,
    And cover thee with maddening spray.

But safe art thou, for strong is He:
    Eternal Love all love will keep:
The sweet shall as the bitter be;
    Thou shalt rejoice as thou dost weep.

CXII.

THE TOMB.

WHAT! is this the only rest
Earth affords her heavenly guest?
For the child she had no room,
To the man she gives—a tomb.

O, Thou weary Man of Love,
Here is stone around, above;
'Tis the dark world's stony heart,
Enter, and fulfil thy part.

Tender linen swathes Thee round,
And a napkin soft is bound
O'er thy features sorrow-worn,
And thy brow so sharply torn.

Such a day deserves its night,
O, sleep on and gather might;
When it pleases Thee to wake,
Tomb and world alike shall shake.

CXIII.

THE STONE.

"Who will roll away the stone?
We are few and are alone,"
Say the women, sad and weak;
"Who will give the help we seek?"

Thus in whispers low they talk,
Sighing on their early walk,
Of the work that has been done
Ere the rising of the sun.

Who will climb into the sky,
Bring redemption from on high?
Who will light the dreary grave,
And the dead and dying save?

All is done that thou wouldst do;
All is finished, soul, for you;
Life is born, and death is dead,
Day is shining, night has fled.

CXIV.

THE SPICES.

THERE is purpose in this waste;
Women, as away ye haste,
Precious spices strew the ground,
Sweetness they will shed around.

What ye meant for him, on us
He has now bestowed, and thus
Sunny winds with fragrant breath
Will disperse the scent of death.

Happy morning, calmly bright,
Never clouds shall dim your light;
Happy garden, kindly free,
All the world may walk in thee.

Love is freer than the wave,
Love is stronger than the grave,
Love is brighter than the sky,
Love has won the victory.

CXV.

PENITENCE.

TO-DAY they "know not what they do;"
  To-morrow, when they see
Their deed, how cruel, must they rue
  Wrong done half-wittingly?

When trembling they for mercy sue,
    Wilt Thou severely say,
" Your hands in blood ye did imbrue ;
    Die, then : " and turn away?

No, that be far from Thee to break
    These penitents so bruised,
Whose hearts for that wild error ache
    They did with minds confused :
Their sin, that made the dull earth shake,
    The speechless heavens grow black,
Thy Mercy quite away can take,
    When Love comes conqueror back,—

Love, stronger than the grave and hell,
    Than fire and frozen death,—
To be Life's cool, eternal well,
    Life's mild, eternal breath.
Sweet sap within the Cross shall swell,
    Green branches round it twine,
That heavenly fruits to earth may tell
    This sorrow was divine.

CXVI.

THE TWO CROWNS.

COME forth with twice-anointed feet,
    And head that waits a second crown,
Thou art more living than the love
    Of those who gently laid Thee down!

Pain is their life, thy grave their cross,
    They grieve, they sigh, they faint for Thee;
Come forth, and make time's bitterest loss
    The joy of their eternity.

Sinner and saint have loved Thee well;
    With ointment pure and purer yet
They have anointed Thee, thy feet
    With heaviest rain of tears were wet:
The sinner wept away her sins,
    The saint held cheap her costly gift;
Arise, Thou lover of both, and each
    To heaven and higher heaven lift.

Crowned but with thorns, thy timid friends
    Who found Thee where to lay thy head,
From secret into open love
    Arose at once when Thou wert dead;
With blood-anointed brow come forth,
    And wear thy shining second crown;
Then into gentleness shall rise
    The world that roughly cast Thee down.

CXVII.

SORROW ENDED.

Arise, sad heart, arise in haste,
    Come forth, but not to weep;
Come, end thy sorrow at the grave
    Where Jesus lay asleep:

He was astir before the sun,
    The stone was rolled away
While darkness yet withheld the dawn,—
    There are two suns to-day.

His servant, day's familiar lord,
    Shall shine no more in vain;
For He, the everlasting sun,
    In flaming power shall reign.
Rise, feeble heart, come quickly forth,
    Though weary night was long;
Let sorrow now be very glad,
    And weakness very strong.

Forget the shudder and the shout,
    The noon with terror black,
That darkly-finished work of woe,—
    The worker has come back;
Himself his finished work, He's here;
    Come, greet the holy light
That flows from sorrow-softened eyes
    With love eternal bright.

Rise, happy heart, arise in haste,
    And into Eden come,
New Paradise is planted now,
    And He, its beauty's sum,
Its tree of life, its light of life,
    Its river of life, is here;
Come, hallow many happy songs
    With one last happy tear.

CXVIII.

JORDAN.

Jordan, O thou crooked river,
    Flowing to the sunken sea,
Filled with lightsome, living waters
    Troubled in lake Galilee;
Ever onward, downward, hasting
    To the abyss whose bitter waves
Soon, the living waters tasting,
    Dying, sink into their graves.

Forth no more thou goest, river,
    From thy grave, the sunken sea;
Breaking through the bars of desert
    Shall a bitter stream go free?
Heavy now thy lightsome waters,
    Salt as penitential tears,
Shed by Israel's sons and daughters,
    Grieving for the wayward years.

Brimming river, ancient river,
    River dear to hearts that love,
Can it be that thou hast perished?
    No, the mighty sun above
To the sea of death is giving
    Vapour's resurrection dress,
And thy waters rising, living,
    Leave behind their bitterness.

Israel, thy course was wayward;
   O, my soul, and so is thine;
But the brightness everlasting
   Makes the dead sea smile and shine;
Though we die because of sinning,
   Falling towards a dark abyss,
Yet our end may be beginning
   Of our rising into bliss.

Arrowy river, happy river,
   He who on Gennesaret's lake
Firmly trod when waves were tossing,
   Calmed their trouble when He spake,
Was He not baptised within thee
   Ruler of the sunken sea?
He has power from death to win thee;
   He has risen, and so shall we.

CXIX.

TRIUMPH.

The glory of God from the way of the East
Shines into the sepulchre, slumber has ceased;
The stone, like a cloud, has moved lightly away,
And on it there sits a strong angel of day.

O, ring, bells of heaven; ye throngs of the blest,
Again hallelujahs may swell from your breast;
Let surges of music, like summer seas bright,
Reëcho and roll through the heavenly height.

They hated and sent Him in darkness to dwell
Beneath the great mountains and billows of hell;
But He lighted the caverns of ancient despair,
And with a new chain bound the fiend in his lair.

He's at liberty set who so sorely was bruised;
He triumphs to-day whom the people refused:
Of all that have loved Him he'll comfort the soul,
Now his own wounded heart is for ever made whole.

And, O, ye kind angels, who grieved for your song,
Sing anew, for the right has prevailed o'er the wrong;
The best of good-will shines through hatred and pain,
And glory and peace have arisen to reign.

CXX.

THE RISEN LORD.

O HAND, O breath divine,
    The helpers of my need;
Lord, let a gift from each be mine,
    Now Thou art risen indeed;
Thy hand, thy very heart,
    Thy lips, were cold and still;
But full of second life Thou art,
    Yet of no second will.

Thy lips are mild and kind,
    The bitterness of death
Has raised in Thee no vengeful mind,
    Nor kindled fiery breath:
Thou art but Jesus weak
    Become omnipotent,
Almightily to do and speak
    Eternal Love's intent.

O, hand that bore the reed,
    O, hand that felt the nail;
Humility is strength indeed,
    And patience shall prevail:
O, breath that deeply sighed,
    O, breath that purely prayed;
With lowest comes the highest tide,
    For joy was sorrow made.

With breath that sighed, inspire;
    With hand once pierced, uphold;
Then, Lord, our courage and desire
    Nor faint shall be nor cold:
All things Thou hast reversed,
    In Thee we rise, not fall;
Thy second life has, through thy first,
    Abolished death for all.

CXXI.

JUDGMENT.

The Apostle spake of judgment just,
    And certain unto men as death;
Prince Felix felt as if the thrust
    Of deadly arrows stayed his breath:
"I'll hear thee at convenient time,"
    He said, his terror to dissemble;
But when can guilt conveniently
    Invite the truth that makes it tremble?

Of Jesus risen, O, news so glad,
    The light of life to nations dead,
The Apostle spake: "Paul, thou art mad,"
    With a loud voice Prince Festus said:
What, will the prince outspeak the voice
    That pierced to Lazarus in his grave,
And stilled the clamouring winds for those
    Who said, "We perish; Jesus, save?"

"Believest thou," the Apostle cried,
    "O King Agrippa, yea, thou dost,
The ancient word?" The king replied,
    "Almost in Christ thou mak'st me trust."
"O, were ye all and wholly his,"
    Said Paul, his fervour shook his chain,
"Not bound as I, but with me free;
    'Almost' is altogether vain."

CXXII.

ASCENSION.

In well-loved blue the heaven shines,
    Familiar heaven, ever dear;
But no array of heavenly signs
    Attests the Lord's departure near;
No flaming chariot hurts the sight,
    No note of trumpet stirs the air;
But pleasant Bethany is bright,
    So full of peace, so free from care.

When last He said, "I go away,"
    A wondering sorrow filled our hearts;
But gladness wonderful to-day
    Shall fill them as the Lord departs:
He lifts those hands so lately torn,
    Whose every touch was health and love,
And, blessing us, is gently borne
    Towards his home of light above.

O grandeur of simplicity!
    Alone, in silence, He ascends;
It is his earthly self we see,
    And downwards still his looks He bends:
The happy angels, kindly wise,
    Their glory hide, their song restrain,
Lest thoughts should in our spirit rise,
    "Alas, we lose, that you may gain."

But while in worship hushed we stand,
    Sweet voices, yet not his, we hear;

Two brother angels are at hand,
    To speak as He shall disappear :
" Ye newly blest, and not bereft,
    On yon fair cloud who gazing stay,
Of king and kingdom is there left
    But this fair cloud, to fade away ?

His home of light, and yours and ours,
    We leave and soon are by your side ;
And have we humble ones such powers,
    What then are his for earth who died ?
Back from the darksome grave He came,
    And back shall come from this bright cloud
In glory of majestic flame,
    With shout, and songs, and trumpet loud."

CXXIII.

BENEDICTION.

He sat upon the mountain side,
    And blest the meek and pure,
And over us to be our guide
    The shining words endure ;
In glory of a peaceful cloud,
    Our pride and sorrow's cure.

And once this ever-glorious man
    Took babes within his arms
To bless them, and He never can
    Abandon us to harms :

This blessing lights the mother's eye,
  Her apprehension calms.

And once the barley-loaves He blest,
  And fishes of the lake,
That multitudes in happy rest
  Their happy fare might take;
This blessing every common meal
  A holy one may make.

And once He said, " O blessed thou,
  Who dost so clearly know
Eternal life is with thee now;
  This doth my Father show."
How blessed they who in the power
  Of this great knowledge grow!

And once He blessed the bread and cup,
  " These are for you," said He;
" Though vines and corn may wither up,
  This blessing's constancy
Will nourish on my truth and love
  All who remember me."

And now in one last blessing He
  All blessings comprehends,
And cheerfully and tenderly
  He gives them to his friends;
That most he may be with us when
  He leaves us and ascends.

CXXIV.

CONDESCENSION.

O Thou whose inmost name is Love,
    Thy double power we know,
The Lord of happiness above,
    And Lord of grief below :
Two centres hast Thou, holy King,
    The heaven and the heart,
Thy world of souls for governing
    With admirable art.

When for the poorest, saddest, worst,
    Thou camest down to die,
The very heart thou enteredst first
    Of all our misery,
Love to Thyself Thou kindlest there
    So comfortably bright,
That in the depth of our despair
    It burns a quenchless light.

O Height, it is the only friend
    That depth can fully bless,
And Thou to us didst condescend
    In utmost lowliness :
Thou hast a centre in our heart,
    The Highest's humble son,
And over grief supreme Thou art,
    And Thou and we are one.

And Depth, unto what other end
  Than height can it aspire?
We rise because Thou didst ascend,
  And still are rising higher:
In Heaven Thou hast a centre too,
  And rayest forth thy power,
That we of pleasures sweet and true
  May reach the crowning hour.

CXXV.

WINDS.

A MIGHTY wind arose in air,
  Commotion swept the world,
And many a heaven-saluting tree
  To earth was roughly hurled;
When forth for havoc, with wide-spreading pinions,
The evil lord raged through his high dominions.

The lord of quarrel and of wrath,
  And unsubmissive will,
Who, seeking joy in boisterous change,
  Continues joyless still;
But let the mimic lord of hosts aërial
Yield to a Prince with power and right imperial.

Lo, spirit against spirit matched,
  The Lord of Peace prevails,
And now the torn and thirsty earth
  Is swept with generous gales;

Musical is the sound of their great rushing,
As on they come, away the dull clouds brushing.

  The Lord of brightness and of warmth,
    Of fragrance and of dew,
  Who having joy in life and growth,
    Finds pleasures ever new;
To herbs the earth, and trees the heaven caressing,
Alike He gives his soft and sunny blessing.

  Hail, mightiest and bounteous wind,
    Distributor of wealth,
  Who giving, comest to confirm
    Or to restore our health;
A blessing thou, bright energy diffusing,
For every other blessing's happiest using.

CXXVI.

RESCUE.

Help, holy Lord, against the league
  Made by the wicked three,
The world, the devil, and the flesh,
  Those foes of sanctity:
O, help, for bitter is the feud,
  And cruel is the hate,
With which they have our souls pursued
  Far forth from Eden's gate.

A while the world is bright and fair,
    The devil smiling stands,
And offering it to tempt the flesh,
    He holds it in his hands;
And then the world is full of woe,
    The flesh of pain and shame,
And evil lurks with flickering tongue,
    Or glares with blinding flame.

Help, holy Wisdom, holy Power,
    O, help, Thou holy Love,
The good against the evil three,
    Who coming from above,
In Christ have fought a rescuing fight,
    The stronger with the strong;
O, help, for still the evil league
    Their vain attempt prolong.

O Spirit, make the flesh of man
    Like flesh of little child,
And form a world by which we may
    Be pleased, but not beguiled;
Kindle the tongues that burn to bless,
    But quench the fires that grieve,
And let the tongue of falsehood cease
    To flicker and deceive.

CXXVII.

THE SUN.

The sun aloft, but not aloof,
    Shines on for evermore;
Makes gold the heavenly roof,
    And green the earthly floor.

His glories flow in ocean streams,
    No ebb can make them less;
First is he, but his beams
    The last and least things bless.

For high and low, and near and far,
    By love can neighbours be;
All heaven has no star
    Too proud for sympathy.

O changeless Lord, celestial sun,
    Who art all souls above,
To make them with Thee one
    In ever-burning love:

In open, ever-during light,
    From ever-shining face;
In ever-serving might,
    And ever-flowing grace:

For heart like Thine, O royal friend,
    How long the world has sighed!
Bring soon to utter end
    The loneliness of pride.

CXXVIII.
HOLY COMMUNION.

I.

Remember us who would aright,
    O Lord, remember Thee,
As on the dark betrayal night
    Shone forth thy constancy.

To Thee, the Truth, O, keep our love
    From worldly leaven pure,
Raising our spirits far above
    Each common threat and lure.

II.

Thy body, like a temple built,
    But wrapt in cold and gloom,
A sanctuary for our guilt,
    Lay silent in the tomb.

Lo, it appears! how full of light,
    Of majesty, of grace,
How wide the gates, how warmly bright
    The open, holiest place!

III.

O Spirit of remembrance, tell
    The tale of Love and Sin;
Their mighty strife, and how He fell,
    Whose was the right to win.

Then, kind interpreter, explain
    How, rising from his fall,
He bore aloft our broken chain,
    And shone the life of all.

IV.

He taught forgiveness, and forgave;
    He prayed, that we might pray;
He said, " Care not your life to save,"
    And gave his own away.

" Seek treasure of unwasting worth,"
    He said, Himself so wise,
That now his vine cheers all the earth,
    His bread the world supplies.

V.

Victorious evermore art Thou,
    The victim of a day;
The thorny crown upon thy brow
    Sends coward fear away.

Thy death was for eternal health,
    Thy shame for endless praise:
O, bleeding hands! the left has wealth,
    The right has length of days.

VI.

If we will live, by love and trust,
    On Him who bore our woes,
Within this body of the dust
    Another body grows.

Its substance like its spirit is;
    For joy's immortal Lord
Makes soul and body such as His
    His gift, and our reward.

VII.

Is Christ divided? Yea, for us
  The one white loaf He breaks;
But every piece is bread, and thus
  Of one strength each partakes.

Is Christ divided? Yea, He parts
  The wine of living red,
That each may drink, and all the hearts
  Be gladdened that are fed.

VIII.

Pure juices sweetened by the skies
  Are in the grass; and, look!
There feeds the lamb for sacrifice
  In meadows by the brook.

Creatures of fierce or gentle kind
  Can be but as they eat;
We all should have a worldly mind
  Without a heavenly meat.

IX.

Lord, when again Thou camest up
  From hell's most darksome gate,
Rememberedst Thou that bitter cup
  Of envy, wrath, and hate?

Thou didst: and giving this for that,
  Thy love, remitting sin,
Said, "Take the cup of life, and at
  Jerusalem begin."

X.

Lord of the stars and spirits seven,
    Celestial breaths and rays;
Thee all the company of heaven
    With love adoring praise.

And we, who eat and drink with Thee,
    Though only on our way
To win the land so bright and free,
    Will love and sing as they.

CXXIX.

UNBELIEF.

We use or waste the beams so bright
    That travel far and swiftly run;
But can there be another light
    Above the brightness of the sun?
A few say Yes; but some say No;
And others say, Can that be so?
But narrow faith enlarges grief;
Help therefore, Lord, our unbelief.

With steam and sails the seas we brave,
    And over billows find our way;
But can the fickle, yielding wave
    Give foothold and commands obey?
A few say Yes; but some say No;
And others say, Can that be so?
But narrow faith enlarges grief;
Help therefore, Lord, our unbelief.

We sometimes sow and nothing reap,
    Or labour much for little bread;
But can a store exhaustless keep,
    And thousands on a loaf be fed?
A few say Yes; but some say No;
And others say, Would that were so
But narrow faith enlarges grief;
Help therefore, Lord, our unbelief.

We tire and sorrow, pine and die,
    Then, Give the earth its earth, we say:
But are there homes within the sky,
    And bright, unwearying, happy day?
A few say Yes; but some say No;
And others say, Ah, were it so!
But narrow faith enlarges grief;
Help therefore, Lord, our unbelief.

O heavenly light and power and peace,
    O bread of life, and life of joy,
Why should we grieve, if grief may cease,
    And death itself alone destroy?
Why? say a few; We must, say some;
And others, *Can* his kingdom come?
But narrow faith enlarges grief;
Help, Lord, O, help our unbelief.

CXXX.

RESURRECTION.

O, THERE are words lips often say,
    They're spoken in the wind and rain,
And heard upon the sunniest day,
    And sweeteners of the bitterest pain;
They're uttered as we're pacing slow
    Towards the dear and holy door,
And when we each of us must go
    The way we've never been before.

And this their burden soft : " I am
    The resurrection and the life;
Mother, I have the little lamb;
    Husband, I have the darling wife;
Young man, I have the honoured maid;
    Maiden, I have the faithful youth :
All, all I have, and I will save;
    I am the way, the life, the truth."

These are thy words, Thou Chief of men,
    O, let them still be sung or said :
But shall we only hear them when
    Sorrowing we carry forth our dead?
Thou speakest thus, each busy day,
    In still voice at the holy dawn,—
" I am the life, the truth, the way ·
    O soul, to this end was I born."

How, Saviour, can the dead be Thine,
    Who living never heard thy voice?
All brightly can their garments shine?
    All sweetly can their hearts rejoice?
How canst Thou those a welcome give,
    Who never cast a care on Thee?
And how can they in honour live
    Who won with Thee no victory?

Souls we'll commit of every kind
    Into thy just and tender hands;
But shall we come to meet Thee blind,
    Or see our Saviour as He stands,
And listening, loving, hear Thee say,—
    Our guide, our champion in the strife,—
"I am thy true ascending way,
    Thy resurrection and thy life?"

CXXXI.

AGE.

A LITTLE sunshine and a little talk,
    Much Bible and much rest upon his chair,
He loved, and often in his tottering walk
    Grandchildren had him in their pretty care.

He sleeps, the old man sleeps: O children, tell,
    How white his hairs, but whiter were his deeds;
Whiter, not fewer: honoured friend, farewell!
    We'll keep our thoughts of thee as precious seeds.

Sown in our hearts they'll yield thee fruits of worth,
    Fruits of thyself in pious deed and word;
Thus back thy younger self shall come to earth,
    And thou in us again be seen and heard.

And more: for lives are new, and men must seek
    Still to be better, and then better still.
Strong fathers would not have their children weak,
    But of yet stronger and yet purer will.

CXXXII.

GONE!

My little flower, my little flower,
    The earth is very dark to me,
Whose love was growing every hour
    The while I watched thy growth and thee.

O broken hope, O breaking heart,
    O baby steps that sound no more,
O prattle hushed: gone, gone thou art,
    My darling, from thy father's door.

Thou playmate of the wind and sun,
    With prettiest foot, and prettier hand;
Quite still thou art, the play is done:
    My God, I *cannot* understand.

And dost thou understand, O man,
    How this fair thing should spring from thee,
So bright, so pure? Such blessing can
    Begotten of thy sorrow be.

Thy flower that bloomed but for a day
    Is now a star, that every night
Shines high in heaven to point thy way
    On to the tearless country bright.

Ah, Lord, then, whether calm or wild
    My night returns, still let me see
My star, my flower, my growing child,
    My baby smiling down on me.

CXXXIII.

EMMANUEL.

Why stooped the Majesty on high?
    Why spake so simply the Allwise?
How came Omnipotence to sigh?
    Why wept the Joy of all the skies?

Shall, then, the Father all things know
    Except the children's want and pain?
And in his heart all sunshine glow,
    Except the sunshine after rain?

And all great things may He perform
    Save greatly fill a humble part?
And rule, but never feel, the storm
    That buffets us in face and heart?

And may He in abstrusest lore
    Teach angels his eternal sway,
But never come to our own door
    To give us comfort for the day?

Day's burden off, its labours done,
    Poor lodging at the weary end
Had He, of gold and silver none,
    A needy man, and all men's friend.

Be glad, the world of toils and scorns
    But perfects Him whom first it mars;
O, love Him for his crown of thorns,
    Then praise Him for his crown of stars.

CXXXIV.

THOROUGHNESS.

Give Him brain and breast,
    And thy ready hand;
He is wisest, best,
    For Him stir or stand.

Give the day and night,
    For Him, trusting, stay;
His arising light
    Show thee will thy way.

Give thyself and thine,
    Life and livelihood,
Still thy less resign
    For his greater good.

Silence give, or word,
    As his need may ask;
Oftener seen than heard,
    Toil thou at thy task.

Give Him cup and plate,
    Fill them with thy best;
Say not, "It is late;
    Trouble not my rest."

Grudge Him not his day,
    In thy spirit search—
Shouldst thou be away
    From thy place at church?

See Him in the street,
    Serve Him in the shop,
Sow with Him thy wheat,
    House for Him thy crop.

Sail with Him at sea,
    Work with Him on land;
Tell Him faithfully
    All that thou hast planned.

Love and learn Him more
    As the common friend;
Joys thou thus shalt store
    For the happy end.

CXXXV.

TESTIMONIES.

IF love in any heart arise,
And stir the tongue, and light the eyes,
And speed the foot, and fill the hand;
Then, Christian, thou must understand
That though unthought of, God is there;
So of denying Him beware.

If Littlemore makes haste to bless
His troubled neighbour Littleless,
And poor men to the poorer give,
Weak ones the weaker help to live,
The sad those sadder still console;
Then God is working in the soul.

If the grown man foregoes his bread
That little mouths may first be fed;

And patient women serve the men
Who care for them but now and then,
And love keeps warm without a fire;
O, then, the grace of God admire.

Two strangers ocean may divide,
Who yet shall bridegroom be and bride,
And God unknown to souls may be
Who love Him will eternally;
But all true hearts our Father knows,
And will to them his truth disclose.

CXXXVI.

DORCAS.

When Dorcas worked to clothe the poor,
    A neighbour or a friend
Sometimes came tapping at the door,
    A little help to lend;
Then Dorcas said, "Come in, my dear;
All willing hands are welcome here."

A friendly light was in her eyes,
    And pity on her tongue,
Her words were mild as well as wise;
    And round her room there hung

Nice things to make the children glad,
And warm ones for the old and sad.

And everybody in the town
    Knew Dorcas, as she went,
In any weather, up and down,
    On doing good intent;
And blest her for her cheerful face,
The kindest woman in the place.

But tender-hearted Dorcas died;
    New tears the widows shed;
For, "Who such garments can provide,
    Now she is gone?" they said;
Dorcas, who by the pleasant sea
Had spent her life so usefully.

She died: they bore her as was meet,
    With many a heavy sigh,
A little further from the street
    And nearer to the sky:
Now in a spacious upper room
She waits the low and narrow tomb.

"O Peter, can she live again?
    This is a grievous day."
Said he, "Submit, and not complain;
    But I will kneel and pray:

'Lord, on thy sorrowing people smile ;
Give Dorcas back a little while.' "

She came : " But not for long," she said ;
   " For God will others raise
Whose lovingkindness, in my stead,
   His gracious name shall praise ;
I heard a voice in Paradise
Say, ' Lovingkindness never dies.' "

And Dorcas in her daughters lives,
   Industrious and kind ;
For help her good example gives
   To willing hand and mind.
Lord, in our hearts her spirit stir :
She followed Thee ; we follow her.

CXXXVII.

THE WANDERER.

I TRAVELLED upwards to the stars,
   And saw a silent glory there ;
I travelled far across the waves ;
   I toiled amid the mountain air ;
The winds they only wailed and sighed,
   And still I bore a burdened mind :
" O, why," I said, " why doth He hide ?
   O, when shall I my Father find ? "

My spirit rose at weary night
    The while I lay upon my bed,
And wandered forth into the dark,
    By thought with glimmering lantern led;
To visit every place I tried
    Which I had seen and left behind:
"O, why," I said, "why doth He hide?
    O, when shall I my Father find?"

I opened many a dusty book,
    And many new ones looked upon;
But all the leaves were wheatless straws,
    And through the dust no sunbeams shone;
And prisoner-like my task I plied,
    The books like bars my soul confined:
"O, why," I said, "why doth He hide?
    O, when shall I my Father find?"

The street has men, the country grass,
    The garden flowers and many a worm,
The past is waste, the future fear,
    The present an uneasy term:
Errors I see on every side,
    But when I look for truth, am blind:
"O, why," I said, "why doth He hide?
    O, when shall I my Father find?"

"Never," a voice said, "if not now,
    And nowhere, if not everywhere:
Return into thyself, for thou
    Art child of hope, and not despair.

One lost and found Him on the cross;
    His love was in the very nails,
His patience in the piercing thorns,
    His pity in the women's wails.

Take thou a splinter of the cross
    And light it at the flaming heart
Of Him who suffered every loss,
    Yea, of the God thou seeking art,
But found Him; and with this bright aid
    Thou find Him shalt thyself within:
O, wandering, weary spirit haste,
    Thy prize thou art about to win."

Hear, silent stars; hear, noisy waves;
    He's found, He's found, my Father's found;
My feet He kisses and He laves;
    'Tis I, He says, am " safe and sound:"
Hence, discontent; away, regret;
    The very worm I will not hate.
He's found; I shall be happy yet;
    My Father says, 'Tis not too late.

I'll kindlier look on men and grass,
    With sunny eyes my books I'll view,
Along my former way I'll pass,
    For all things now are very new:
I thank thee, Gospel, for that word;
    O, I had wandered far around:
I lost Him in the universe,
    But in my heart my Father's found.

CXXXVIII.

HELP IS SURE.

As one who for a letter waits
   From loving kindred far away,
Who dwell at home, still hesitates
   "They have forgotten me" to say;
Even so will faith our hearts restrain
From saying, I have prayed in vain.

Could but the eyes that grow so dim
   Beside a solitary fire,
Look forth beyond the horizon's rim,
   And see the coming ship—Desire;
Up like a flame the heart would leap,
Although slow hours their watch must keep.

We live by faith, but God by sight;
   He sees the heart; help too He sees,
Which, travelling onward through the night,
   Will on the morrow give us ease;
He prompts the praying to endure,
Because his promised help is sure.

While the root, locked in slumber fast,
   Rests through the weary winter-tide,
The world speeds on, that God at last
   His summer's heartsease may provide,
And all love's tender prophecies
In tenderer blooms may realise.

CXXXIX.

PATRIOTISM.

TOGETHER for our Country now we pray;
Give her good speed upon her ancient way;
And for her broadening world a brighter day,
Till all men prosper that her laws obey.

God save the Queen! and all of honoured name!
May virtue shine in them with steadfast flame;
Let worthy deeds inspire the tongue of fame,
And flaring falsities be quenched in shame.

God save the Church! may all good men combine,
As from one root may many branches shine;
And rich in unadulterate loaves and wine,
May lessening want and woe declare her Thine.

God save the people and their houses all,
The thriving, striving, and both great and small!
And let us on thy love with one voice call,
When the sun rises, and the shadows fall.

CXL.

INTERCESSION.

WE come, but not with sighs alone,
  Nor only with confession;
Nor but as suppliants to thy throne,
  To win some new possession;

But with adoring homage, Lord,
    And spirit triumphing,
To pity rich and wisdom deep
    A prayerful song we bring.

To Thee, sweet mercy's ancient fount,
    We now come interceding,
For spirits more than we can count,
    Who mercy's help are needing;
No love of men for man with Thine
    For all men can compare;
And vast and varied as the world,
    So large shall be our prayer.

We pray for glad men and for grieved,
    That, one another knowing,
The sorrowful may be relieved,
    The happy happier growing;
For men who wander and who rest,
    That, venturing from home,
The brave may find and rescue those
    That in the deserts roam.

For people who on beds of pain,
    Or on the waves, are tossing,
That they their home or heaven may gain,
    The seas or river crossing;
For cottagers, who, mid the corn,
    Have still but scanty store;
And those who toil in wealthy towns,
    And yet continue poor.

For men of less or larger trade,
    The ship's or shoulder's burden,
That trust and love and coin be made
    For them a triple guerdon;
We pray for rulers and the ruled,
    For teachers and the taught;
For all who weave the triple cord
    Of art and truth and thought.

For busy men of all pursuits,
    All colours and conditions,
That thorny cares may yield sweet fruits,
    And comforts be physicians;
For all who are for freedom bound,
    For all who get to give,
Or suffer wrong to strengthen right,
    And die that men may live.

For those who, having erred and sinned,
    Are maddened with their trouble,
And think the truth a fickle wind,
    The solid world a bubble;
Who call eternal life a guess,
    The Gospel but a tale;—
That hope may blossom in the dust,
    And penitence prevail.

For those whose breath is now a sigh,
    Whose love with pains is smarting;
For those who soothe the infant's cry,
    Or watch old age departing;

To Thee an ever-widening prayer
    Adoringly we bring,
That strength from weakness, joy from pain,
    And wealth from want may spring.

CXLI.

MARRIAGE.

HEART with heart and hand in hand,
    Go upon your way;
Pleasant is the promised land
    You're entering to-day;
        Corn it has and wine,
            Fields for work and play;
        On it love divine
            Sheds benignant ray.

Love the Lord of love, ye two,
    He has made you one;
He's the home-adviser who
    Is welcome as the sun;
        Shows you by his light
            What to seek and shun;
        Stays beside you quite
            Till your work is done.

Husband, all your husbandry
    For love's sake pursue;
Wife, let love your magnet be
    To draw him back to you:

Love makes little much
    When our joys are few,
And when most, his touch
    Gives them golden hue.

Heart with heart and hand in hand,
    O, give thanks and pray;
On a sunny height you stand,
    A new scene to survey:
        In your bower of bliss
            Though you cannot stay,
        Love need never miss
            Either work or way.

CXLII.

INFANT BAPTISM.

PRAYING by the river-side,
From the heaven serenely wide,
To Thee, Saviour, came the dove,
Fullest life of peace and love.

And he came not as a guest,
Thou art his eternal rest,
O, Thou holiest abode
Of the inmost life of God.

Saviour, now this infant bless
As with a divine caress;
Make this little heart thy home,
To it with thy spirit come.

Soft as water on the brow,
Softly, gently, comest Thou;
But hast gifts for every hour,
Purity and peace and power.

On the dark, tempestuous day,
Lord, Thou hastenedst not away;
But didst face the roughest wind,
Carrying forth thy message kind.

Faith and hope and holy love,
Wings and spirit of the dove,
Father, on this babe bestow;
Like the Saviour may he grow.

CXLIII.

BABY.

O BABY, He loved pretty things;
   "Consider the lilies," said He:
Thy mother, she sighs or she sings,
   But still she's considering thee.

O baby, He loved little birds;
   "Not one is forgotten," said He:
Thy mother remembers his words,
   And comforts herself about thee.

In graces, thy mother hath prayed—
　Since daily her baby she drest—
Thou mayst like the flower be arrayed,
　Which Jesus admired and blest.

O, dove, from the heavens that shine,
　Whose home is his merciful breast;
Come visit this baby of mine,
　My new little bird in its nest.

CXLIV.

LET CHILDREN COME.

Let children come;
Love has made all ready;
　Our Father's arms
How strong they are, how steady;
　'Tis He that gives
This pure and pleasant water,
　And to Him lives
Each little son and daughter.

Let children come;
To each heart so tender,
　Drops as from heaven,
Their blessing soft shall render;
　Dear budding plant,
Thy God for thine unfolding
　His love will grant,
Our love for thee beholding.

Let children come,
This our love God gave us,
Who gave his Son,
From hate and fear to save us;
For all life's thirst
Of water He's the river,
Who from the first
Of pure life is the giver.

CXLV.

WAVES.

My soul, humility her fears have taught her;
She said, "Lord, bid me come upon the water;"
And would have sunk, Lord, but Thou didst support her.

For, O, the wild-faced waves her path surrounding,
Leaped at her, all with wrathful voices sounding;
She failed, she cried, her terrors were confounding.

But thy great love her little faith not scorning,
Made shame but as a dream, her pride for warning;
Then bade the dream begone, and it was morning.

To quell the waves! such task Thou didst not set her;
To toil on them, and trust, for her is better;
And in her perils Thou wilt not forget her.

CXLVI.

THE SOWER.

O, DAY of rest for busy men,
    We welcome thee once more;
And look towards the truth as when
    The people on the shore
Looked towards the Saviour on the lake,
A boat the pulpit whence He spake.

Lord, bid those wandering winds be still,
    That rob us of thy word;
Then lessons of thy heavenly will
    Shall from the boat be heard:
The boat, for work and peril made,
Says, "Be not idle nor afraid."

Behold the sower comes again,
    Our heart it is the ground;
He bears the plenteous living grain,
    And scatters it around:
The frequent foot, the stony soil,
The ready weeds, his labour spoil.

O, blessed owner of the field,
    Sower of truth alone,
Our hearts must love the truth, to yield
    Its increase as thine own;
Therefore, O Lord, prepare our heart
To cherish what Thou shalt impart.

True Lord alike of toil and rest,
    Not yet may labour cease;
So we will work and dare our best,
    Else on the day of peace
Our heart with trouble will be weak
When from the boat we hear·Thee speak.

CXLVII.

EXHORTATION.

THE Lord is rich and merciful,
    The Lord is very kind;
O, come to Him, come now to Him,
    With a believing mind.
His comforts they shall strengthen thee,
    Like flowing waters cool;
And He shall for thy spirit be
    A fountain ever full.

The Lord is glorious and strong,
    Our God is very high;
O, trust in Him, trust now in Him,
    And have security.
He shall be to thee like the sea,
    And thou shalt surely feel
His wind, that bloweth healthily,
    Thy sicknesses to heal.

The Lord is wonderful and wise,
    As all the ages tell;

O, learn of Him, learn now of Him,
  Then with thee it is well.
And with his light thou shalt be blest,
  Therein to work and live;
And He shall be to thee a rest
  When evening hours arrive.

CXLVIII.

RAIN.

One blessing is there of the sun,
  Another of the rain;
Two blessings better are than one,
  Though often we complain,
And wish the one we have away,
Or given to-morrow, not to-day.

To-day the pleasant light is less,
  The busy rain descends,
The sky is in its working dress,
  And needy earth befriends;
But less the light, not less the love,
Now all the heaven is dark above.

Bright o'er the earth a brazen sky
  Burnt when the people sinned;
But heaven when their relief was nigh
  Grew black with clouds and wind;
A mighty rain that mercy sent,
Which called the people to repent.

Too fervently the sun may shine,
    Rain fall too heavily;
But still their lesson is divine—
    A better world shall be,
Where everything will only bless,
And everyone work righteousness.

Lord, we are Thine, and Thou art ours,
    Thine too are sun and rain,
And Thou for us their varying powers,
    Wilt heighten or restrain;
Then be the weather what it will,
We trustfully will serve Thee still.

CXLIX.

MATINS.

CREATOR, lover of the whole,
Our prayer for body and for soul,
O, hear; invigorate and control,
                  Within us move.
As hidden springs their presence tell,
When from within the waters swell,
By overflowings of the well,
                  So Thou thy love.

The lark ascends on wing so strong,
He carols in the heavens long,
Then touches earth, and ends his song,
                  Fresh for his care.

And so to Thee we singing rise
And overflow in melodies;
Then downward come refreshed and wise,
                To work and bear.

For us the powerful morning rose,
For us the solemn sunset glows
How soon! then darkening heavens disclose
                Their starry wealth.
O, for a heart to sing and serve,
A will that not again would swerve;
O, for the thrilling, steadfast nerve
                Of perfect health!

To study and possess the earth
Is ours by privilege of birth;
And ours to find the hidden worth
                Of nature's store.
Ours too the sinew and the limb
To climb the height, the depth to swim;
For all we thank Thee in our hymn,
                Yet ask for more.

O heavenly Lord, whose mercy can,
By power and prudence of thy plan,
Both slay the sins and save the man,
                So wise thy way;
Now give us of his heart and powers
Who chose the thorn, yet loved the flowers,
And filled for us the twelve sad hours
                Of his great day.

Ours be the love by which He wept
For others' grief, yet onward kept;
Nor quailed upon the way, nor slept,
    To his dark cross.
Then on the highway, in the mart,
While still we bear a brother's part,
We shall compute with heavenly art
    Our gain and loss.

CL.

REPLIES.

How can I sing?
 The sullen hours,
With heavy wing
 And drooping powers,
Bear me slowly on,
And I fail anon.

How can I sing?
 Of what? To whom?
Cold shadows cling
 Round church and tomb;
Thoughts of God and death
Stop alike my breath.

How can I sing?
 The time is gray:
Deceiving spring
 Has passed away:

Look, the fields are bare,
Sown with fruitless prayer.

Sing, do but sing;
   The kindly hours,
With lighter wing
   And livelier powers,
Bear thee swiftly on;
Thou art home anon.

Sing, thou must sing,
   Of life: to God:
Dawn will He bring
   To spire and sod:
Thoughts of God and rest
Are alike thy best.

Sing, thou canst sing,
   Young-hearted, gay
Summer shall fling
   Thy doubts away:
Look, new hopes arise,
Seedlings of the skies.

CLI.

HEAVEN.

Arising, we sing
   To Jesus on high,
And give our thoughts wing
   From earth to the sky;

Where millions at ease
  Tell in bright fields of air
Of toils on the seas,
  And of earth with its care.

No threat'ning nor taunt
  Can darken their heart;
Upbraiding and vaunt
  No friendships can part:
Time loses his scythe
  When he enters the skies;
Old people are blithe,
  And the young ones are wise.

None take with a smile
  But give with a groan;
None think it worth while
  To lock up their own:
But lovingly, merrily,
  All the days fly;
And verily, verily,
  No one shall die.

The fruits that were rare
  Are had for a wish;
Flowers holy and fair
  Give grace to the dish;
The thistle and thorn
  As mementos are shown
Of griefs that were borne
  Ere love's triumph was known.

Then sing, sing anew,
    To Jesus above;
His words were all true,
    His work was all love.
With holy behaviour
    Let trouble be braved,
We work with the Saviour,
    To rest with the saved.

The weary shall rest,
    The sufferers sing;
Those pains are the best
    Such pleasures that bring.
No labour is sorrow
    But labour in vain;
In hope, then, to-morrow
    We'll labour again.

CLII.

BIRTH.

God of the shining sun,
Each little life begun
    On our dark earth
Appears because thy will,
Which doth all heaven fill
With pleasures free from ill,
    Allows the birth.

Not with unjoyful care
Nor with unpraiseful prayer
   We live below;
Assailed by pain and sin,
We yet are born to win
The holy heaven wherein
   No evils grow.

God of the peaceful height,
Thy word of promise bright
   Spans the rough sea;
A rainbow fair to view,
As broad as bright of hue,
And all souls may come through,
   Travelling to Thee.

O Spirit, Father, Son,
Thou glorious threefold one,
   Blest be thy name;
Thy word that must endure,
And love for ever pure,
And patient power, insure
   Our rise from shame.

CLIII.
SYMPATHY.

Not afar from surf and wave
Thou didst speak the word and save,
But while tossing on the sea
Didst command tranquillity.

Not upon us from the skies
Didst Thou look with happy eyes,
But while sorrowing with us here
Thou didst shed the pitying tear.

Not with trumpet from a rock
Didst Thou guide the battle's shock,
But in front of us didst go,
And receive the heaviest blow.

Not alone the just man's friend,
Worthy lives didst Thou commend;
But to those who sinned before
Saidst Thou, "Go, and sin no more."

Thine the black and bitter bread,
Thine the busy, weary head,
Thine the ready, aching feet,
Thine the burden and the heat.

Worth the myriads of us,
Didst Thou live and labour thus,
Saviour, and shall we refuse
Everything that Thou didst choose?

CLIV.

THE BREAD OF LIFE.

Bread art Thou by thy coming down
    To teach and grieve, and die ;
And wine by thine ascent and crown,
    Joy, power, and victory.

Thy parables are bread, O Lord,
    Made of the finest wheat ;
Their plenty in thy word is stored,
    That every man may eat.

Thy miracles are gladdening wine
    Of consolation strong,
To cheer us with a hope divine
    Our weary way along.

No more is earth a common thing,
    But full of meaning bright ;
Each work can for a higher bring
    A clear and heavenly light ;

And of our own awaiting life
    The holy wonders tell,
When will and world no more at strife,
    All will be miracle.

Then let us eat and drink, and thus
    Gain vigour for our way ;
And happy will it be for us,
    As all the Scriptures say.

CLV.

OFFERINGS.

When fragrantly towards the skies
Ascends the noblest sacrifice,
And God is honoured perfectly,
Four contributions there must be :
The common earth yields dust and stone,
The blood and flesh these are our own,
Unfriendly hearts cold water bring,
Heaven's fire completes the offering.

Spirit of love, we lay our best
Upon the hard earth's stony breast,
Drenched with the lavish unbelief
Of many round : our faith and grief
Accept; change shadow into light;
Let fire, with ruddy ardour bright,
Through flesh and stone and water shine;
Thus glorify Thyself and Thine.

CLVI.

WAITING.

While waiting for the summer sun,
   The winter fire is warm and bright;
And though to-morrow's dawn is sure,
   A lamp we kindle for to-night.

O Book of Life, thou art my lamp;
  Thy beam how friendly and how clear!
By waters sounding in the dark
  I travel on, and will not fear.

And oft I rest in shelter safe,
  And feel the fire's kindly glow,
Thy church my home; thy promise, Lord,
  Still brightest when the dark storms blow.

Take comfort, then, my soul, and wait
  For all thy Saviour said should come;
That summer and that day so great,
  The last and lasting light and bloom.

CLVII.

THE PRIZE.

"A BUBBLE I would be," says one;
"O, let me perish in the sun,
As brightly end as I begun!
It is not nothingness I shun,
For dark the course that I must run,
No prize can at the end be won."

And why, O doubting soul and sad,
May any one but thou be glad?
And why by thee no prize be had?
One is there, O how brightly clad!
Dark was his way, is thine as bad?
Let not much sorrow make thee mad.

Within the egg how darkly lies
Even the bird of paradise,
Predestined for the sunniest skies!
Yet forth it comes, away it flies,
How brightly, swiftly will it rise,
Its happy life the parents' prize!

Bubble and egg to teach combine:
To be a bubble wilt thou pine?
The breaking egg—be that thy sign:
Thou shalt begin, not cease, to shine;
Over thee broods the love divine;
Thou art its prize, and it is thine.

CLVIII.

ADMONITION.

ONE sat with angry heart alone,
    And thought on sin and thought on care;
Too vexed with self for any work—
    Too dull and undevout for prayer.
Sudden he said, "I will go forth;"
    And, lo, the evening was so fair,
So bright, so seriously kind,
    Forgiveness rested in the air,
Holiness moved upon the wind,
And round about, from south to north,
    Prevailing love shone everywhere.

"Then why," said he, "O, why, my Lord,
    Sat I in sin when Thou wert here,

Awaiting me with health and hope,
    Willing to cleanse me and to cheer?
This beauty calms my peevish soul;
    Light tells me conscience may be clear;
The air's cool touch hath made me strong,
    The silence whispers, 'Thou art dear,
Still dear to God; thou didst Him wrong;
He loves thee, for He makes thee whole:
    O, be not slave of any fear.'"

CLIX.

EXULTATION.

Sometimes God lights his temple up
    With an exceeding sanctity,
And as from sacramental cup,
    That brims with wine of Jubilee,
The golden king and silver queen
    Proffer that blissful love below
Which hath with God for ever been,
    And will from God for ever flow.

O, day most beauteous of the days,
    O, night most solemn of the nights,
Beneath your temple-roof I raise
    Eyes brimming with divine delights;
And pledge my God, who pledges me,
    That I will serve, will love Him more;
I drink his own felicity,
    And thrilling gratefully adore.

Like coloured wings cherubical,
    Whose glancings variegate the home
Where spirits ever-happy dwell,
    Where no unholy darkness comes,
Ye clouds, sail gently, gently shine;
    O, when like you shall I arise,
For sports and services divine,
    Full-winged with sinless energies?

I rise, O mighty God, I rise,
    I'm rising as in heart I kneel;
And, O, ye solemn, loving skies,
    Echo around the thanks I feel;
Ye sun and moon, be witnesses
    That I, a man by God made free,
His name with kindling spirit bless
    And soaring joys of jubilee.

CLX.

FORGET NOT.

FORGET not: can the mother's love
    Grow cold towards her child;
Or children quite forget the voice
    So earnest and so mild;
Or wanderers about the world,
    Who many things have seen,
Forget their village and its brook,
    The garden and the green?

Forget not: can the lark forget
    The songs so often sung;
Or mighty eagles to supply
    With food their callow young;
The wearied bee forget to sip
    The honey from the flower;
The candle-braving moth forget
    To shelter from the shower?

Forget not: can the fly forget
    Its gambols in the sun;
The summer-staying birds forget
    The winter's force to shun;
Or white-winged ocean-birds forget
    The water's murmurous roar;
Or busy ants unmindful grow
    Of work and house and store?

Wilt thou forget thy holiest love,
    Thine earliest sigh and song;
The truth that guarded thee when weak,
    To prosper thee when strong;
Thy purpose pure; the innocence
    That sweetened work and play;
The light that makes this dark world safe,
    And shows our heavenly way?

CLXI.

SLEEP.

Giver of sleep, unsleeping Lord,
Now am I to my chamber come;
Where flesh and heart each seek their home;
Thy nightly gift again I crave,
My wearied frame repose would have;
My heart the promise of thy word.

Just ready to depart, the Day
Spake to me in my garden walk,
Where oft the Day and I do talk,
And said, " O Soul, both thou and I
Have lived beneath a Father's eye;
And now to Him I go away."

Then soon the Night, immense with stars,
Whose gentle and immortal flame
Burns on in sanctity the same
As when Thou first didst light their fires,
Came, saying, " O Soul, are thy desires
Bound to the earth by sensual bars?"

Not unrebukable am I,
Not spotless thy command have kept;
Yet, Lord, my day's poor work accept,
For I have lived as in thy view;
Accept that wistful worship too
Wherewith I gave the Night reply.

Here now I am: the house is fast;
I am shut in from all but Thee;
Great witness of my privacy,
Dare I unshamed my soul undress,
And, like a child, ask thy caress,
Thou Ruler of a realm so vast?

Ask it I will; I cannot rest
Unless Thou grant some tender sign,
Assuring me that I am Thine:
The mightiest king that father is
Loves well his little ones to kiss;
And art not Thou of fathers best?

Of fathers best, of kings supreme,
Child of the kingdom reckon me,
With Jesus one, thus born of Thee,
Secured and nourished by his grace,
And righteous in his righteousness—
Say, "Ever thou art mine in Him."

The light is out: my rest I'll take;
Down with unfearing heart I lie,
And wait sleep's healing mystery,—
Still as the grave, but kind as heaven:
Such sleep, O Lord, to me be given,
That I may holier, stronger wake.

CLXII.

SIGNS.

Lift up your heads, rejoice,
    Redemption draweth nigh;
Now breathes a softer air,
    Now shines a milder sky;
The early trees put forth
    Their new and tender leaf;
Hushed is the moaning wind
    That told of winter's grief.

Lift up your heads, rejoice,
    Redemption draweth nigh;
Now mount the laden clouds,
    Now flames the darkening sky;
The early scattered drops
    Descend with heavy fall,
And to the waiting earth
    The hidden thunders call.

Lift up your heads, rejoice,
    Redemption draweth nigh;
O, note the varying signs
    Of earth, and air, and sky;
The God of glory comes
    In gentleness and might,
To comfort and alarm,
    To succour and to smite.

He comes the wide world's king,
    He comes the true heart's friend,
New gladness to begin,
    And ancient wrong to end;
He comes to fill with light
    The weary, waiting eye :
Lift up your heads, rejoice,
    Redemption draweth nigh.

CLXIII.

TEMPEST.

WITH many a swift and crashing stroke
    From clouds, the frigates of the sky,
Huge, solemn-sailing clouds, there broke
    Victorious bursts of energy.

The lance-like rain, the darting hail,
    These rushed and ceased, while round about
The sulphurous lightnings, red or pale,
    Gleamed and led on the rolling shout.

I saw the glorious battle-show,
    The Lord came down, and for us fought;
Blights and diseases were the foe;
    Great was the victory He wrought.

Now breathes a tranquil, buoyant air;
    Nature oppressed is calm and free;
O storm, thy sounds of terror were
    The signals of thy victory.

One general pleasure of release
    Pervades to-day the earth and sky;
Bright, quiet clouds, like ships of peace,
    The airy ocean beautify.

While anchored on the horizon far,
    Dark, battle-broken clouds attest
The sharpness of that heavenly war
    By which they purchased us our rest.

CLXIV.

PLEADING.

APPEAR, O Thou, who very present art,
    In rest to comfort, and in action guide,
Those who to Thee all-willingly impart
    This heavy task—their deep want to provide.

I know that secretly Thou workest, Lord,
    But openly reveal thy wisdom kind;
With thy sweet light my spirit turn toward,
    As still my spirit turns toward Thee, blind.

Open my vision, and unlock the limbs
    That know they live, yet in sad palsy lie;
When on a windless sea life's vessel swims,
    Becalmed, afraid, my God, to Thee I cry.

Profound art Thou in thy salvation, Lord;
   Most subtly inward is thy holy work;
I know thy treasures are within me stored,
   But, ah, what spoilers still within me lurk!

O, save me from the dark, deceiving worm,
   Which wastefully devours what Thou hast given;
Save from that spoiler the engrafted germ
   Of thy right will, which angels do in heaven.

CLXV.

ANGELS.

How holy and secure those angels kind,
   Whose gentleness the struggling church assists;
Possessors ever of an open mind,
   Free to the sun, untroubled with dark mists.

They seeing, know the ever-shining source
   Of being and its blessedness, the Lord;
And in communion of life's hallowed force
   They take and give, they ask and have thy word.

O Thou one Lord, in Thee such being is
   That from Thee million spirits have their name;
Still Thou providest them with changing bliss,
   That still to Thee their love may higher flame.

What heaven so high, but love is still beyond?
    What hell so deep, that love is not below?
What length of times bemused by fancy fond,
    What breadth of countries has the world to show,

Such that love is inadequate to fill,
    To reach, to brighten, and to reconcile?
All in the all is Love, and hidden still
    It opens with a new and heightened smile.

CLXVI.

ONE FAMILY. Eph. iii. 14, 15.

HERE are we dark and weak, yet are we not
    Excluded from thy glorious family;
Pain to thy children is a transient lot;
    We suffer, that from sin we may be free.

Angels and men, the prophet and the child,
    These all are what they are by gift of Thine;
No break or gulf is there; the undefiled
    Are tenderly made one by birth divine.

If but a letter of the all-perfect name,
    If but a mark of the celestial pen,
Distinguish us, we will, despising shame,
    Abjuring self, live boldly among men.

Named after God! a little like to Him,
  In whom the entireness of the name divine
Brightly involved was once by woes made dim,
  But now unfolded shines, yet more to shine.

Only by Christ can Jesus be explained,
  My Lord, my God, O, may I yet become
An image of the love whence I have gained
  The initial figure of an endless sum.

Thou who in Jesus wert in Jesus art;
  My present Saviour art Thou; therefore I
Seek life from Thee through Him, that my new heart
  Of and for Him and hope may testify.

CLXVII.

RESTORATION.

How sweet to me is life when shadows gray
  Threaten a sunset to my spirit's sun!
I would not into memory sink away,
  And weary dreams of work too sadly done.

Return in light; faith to my faith impart,
  Love to my love, and eyesight to my eyes,
Life to my life, and motion to my heart,
  Nerve to my arms, and to these victories.

Restore my joys, let sweetly rippling peace
  Be in the stead of dark, stagnating calm;
In truth of thy salvation, O, release
  My bondaged spirit from engirding harm.

So act in me that I from Thee may act,
  Free with a liberty Thou hast inspired;
Then, like a broken city recompact,
  My heart shall fortress be and home desired.

O, fill me with the energy that filled
  Thine own dark days, Great Master, with success,
Sustaining Thee, as still thy mercy willed
  To share, and so subdue, the world's distress.

Then, then, with sweetening words for others' taste,
  And ever-strengthening interior might,
I'll give the weary drink, and onward haste
  Towards thy dear mansion of unclouded light.

L'Envoi.

O Book! the birth of winter days,
First fostered by the genial rays
    Of winter's household fire;
Growing through summer-tide and spring,
When other leaves were withering
    Thou hadst thy full attire.

A sanctity is in thy page,
That thou mayst cheer the pilgrimage
    That weary mortals know;
For dusky earth can take a light
From verses pure, as doth the night
    From new-descended snow.

I said: Go forth and face the years,
Tremble no more with modest fears,—
    With love thou shalt be blest:
If any greet thee with disdain,
Suffer, but not parade, thy pain,
    And meekly do thy best.

Go, like a bark, nor fear the sea;
Thy haven shall the approval be
    Of hearts with faith like thine;
Thou on Time's waters shalt prevail;
If breath of heaven fills the sail,
    Heaven's smiles upon it shine.

L'ENVOI.

O Book! If any show thee slight,
Thou knowest with pain and with delight
    Thou of the heart wast born;
Hast in thee life of shade and shower,
Of sunny and of starry hour,
    Of evening and of dawn.

If any call thee beautiful,
O, haste and of the glories tell
    That in the temple wait;
For thou, if golden light divine
Upon thee from love's altar shine,
    Art but a temple-gate.

Sweet is the brier on summer morns
When the fresh leaves, concealing thorns,
    Exhale life's tenderness:
Happy the sorrowing heart at times
When truths that pierce, in pleasant rhymes
    Their virtues can express.

The sweetnesses of love that dwell
In truth, by language musical
    Alone can uttered be;
And thoughts have goodliest blossoming
When they grow nearest to the spring
    Of sacred poesy.

L'ENVOI.

A little while, and he who sung,
With silenced voice and harp unstrung
   In quiet earth shall lie ;
Ah, will he then attain his home?
Will beautiful and blest ones come
   And guide him up the sky?

Mother, so simple yet so sage,
A troubled youth thy patronage
   Enjoyed, and thine alone ;
And dost thou visit still thy son,
And love the work that he has done,
   And count it as thine own?

Inspiring Saviour, unto Thee
My work I give in fealty,
   Thy life I have and seek :
Accept my sacrifice of song ;
Weak am I,—but if therefore strong,
   O, keep me ever weak !

Book! if the thanks of simple hearts
Be thine, because thy song imparts
   To them the power to sing ;
Offer with theirs thy thanks to Him
To whom the saintliest seraphim
   The lowliest homage bring.

November, 1855.

3

www.ingramcontent.com/pod-product-compliance
Lightning Source LLC
Chambersburg PA
CBHW031818230426
43669CB00009B/1184